Dealing with

DIFFICULT

PEOPLE

PROVEN STRATEGIES FOR
HANDLING STRESSFUL SITUATIONS
AND DEFUSING TENSIONS

ROBERTA CAVA

PIATKUS

*Dedicated to those seminar participants
who have had to deal with difficult people
and have passed on their ideas so others
might benefit from their experience.*

Copyright © 1990 by Roberta Cava

This edition first published in Great Britain in 1990 by
Judy Piatkus (Publishers) Ltd of
5 Windmill Street, London W1P 1HF

Reprinted 1991
Reprinted 1992 (twice)
Reprinted 1993

Published in Canada in 1990
by Key Porter Books, Ltd

The moral right of the author has been asserted

British Library Cataloguing in Publication Data

Cava, Roberta
   Dealing with difficult people: how to improve your
   communication skills in the workplace.
   1. Personnel. Communication skills. Development
   I. Title
   302.2

   ISBN 0–7499–1019–4
   ISBN 0–7499–1091–7 (Pbk)

Design: Scott Richardson
Printed and bound in Great Britain by
Mackays of Chatham PLC, Chatham, Kent

CONTENTS

ACKNOWLEDGEMENTS

My gratitude is extended to the thousands of participants of my seminars who contributed ideas on how they handled their difficult people.

Special thanks go to Alberta Government Telephones who let me quote directly from several of their brochures, and my editor, Margaret Allen.

Thanks to my mother, Mabel Hastie, who taught me patience and stick-to-it-iveness, and to my daughter, Michele, who tolerated the many hours of isolation writing this book demanded of me.

INTRODUCTION

Do you have to deal with irate, rude, impatient, emotional, persistent or aggressive people? Do you come home from work stressed out from having had to deal with difficult people all day? If so, reading this book will enable you to control your moods by not allowing others to give you negative feelings. You'll learn how to control your anger and stress levels and obtain a psychological edge by improving your people skills.

Businesses (especially those offering services) are learning the importance of having employees who are capable of handling all types of difficult people and situations. Employees who succeed in this area are in great demand.

Difficult people are the ones who try to:
— make us lose our cool;
— force us to do things we don't want to do;
— prevent us from doing what we want or need to do;
— often use coercion, manipulation or other underhanded methods to get their way;
— make us feel guilty if we don't go along with their wishes;
— make us anxious, upset, frustrated, angry, depressed, jealous, inferior, defeated or any other negative feeling;
— make us do their share of the work.

Knowing techniques *that work* for dealing with difficult people and situations can boost your confidence, improve your competence at work, reduce stress and anxiety and increase your enthusiasm for your job.

You'll experience a feeling of accomplishment when you handle difficult situations well. Your employer, co-workers and staff will trust and rely on you, will admire and like you, will think twice before pushing you around and will be more willing to try to please you.

How do I know that the techniques outlined in this book really *work*? Because more than 10,000 participants have attended my seminar and have given their input. Many took the time to write to me with examples of how they dealt with particularly difficult situations. These contributions are scattered throughout the book. I endorse every technique described here and use them regularly. Not only do I handle difficult situations better, but I've gained control of my reactions to negative situations. So can you!

CHAPTER ONE

CHAPTER

UNDERSTANDING BEHAVIOUR AND ITS EFFECTS

Question: What is a difficult person? *Answer*: A person whose behaviour causes difficulties — for you and others. Dealing with difficult people simply means dealing with difficult *behaviour*.

This book is about the interaction between you and others. Interaction is a two-way street. You react to a person: the person reacts to you. We may not be able to control other people's behaviour directly but, by learning how to manage our own behaviour and developing techniques for communicating effectively, we can influence other people in a positive way. We can turn their (and our own) difficult behaviour into civilized, constructive behaviour that allows both us and others to think well of ourselves.

Learning to deal with difficult people involves learning how to manage *your* side of a two-way transaction. This gives the other person a chance to work with you to resolve whatever is making him or her difficult.

When we encounter a difficult person, many of us react in ways that make the problem worse — for example, by making a sharp retort, by becoming defensive rather than attempting to deal with the real issue, by taking the person's anger personally. These natural but counterproductive responses reduce our chances of transforming a negative encounter into a constructive one.

For example, many times, when you are dealing with people who are irritable, rude, impatient or angry, you're not in a position to yell back. This is especially true if you work on the front lines for your company and run into difficult people either on the phone or in person. You can control your negative reaction if you mentally refuse to accept the negatives they're throwing at you.

Suppose that a client starts to bawl you out, really takes a strip off you for something that wasn't your fault. What would your natural reaction be?

1. *You defend yourself or your company.*

Most of us respond this way. The client attacked you verbally, which triggered your defence mechanism. This response is instinctive, as natural for you as breathing. When you respond defensively, does it usually solve anything? Not likely. Is this going to satisfy the customer? Not likely. You could end up in a shouting match, with negative feelings for both parties.

2. *You're furious at the client's behaviour, but grit your teeth and concentrate on solving the problem.*

You've allowed the situation to get to you. This is also a negative response — in this case, for you. Stop for a moment and ask yourself, "What is the client mad at — me or the situation?" In most cases, it's the situation. You happen to be there, so you become the recipient of the client's frustration and anger.

3. *Before responding, you take time to recognize that the client is angry at the situation, not at you. Therefore, there's no need for you to defend yourself.*

This last solution works best. You accomplish this by stopping your defence mechanism from kicking in. It's easier to do this than you think. It takes practice — but you can do it if you set your mind to it! As soon as you feel yourself getting uptight and feel the need to defend yourself — stop and analyse the situation. The customer is upset at your company or the situation — not at you. There is absolutely no need for you to defend yourself. Instead, you can concentrate on solving the client's problem. The client ends up happy and so do you — a win-win situation.

You might think it's wimpy to handle situations this way, but the end result is positive for both parties. You choose the correct approach by concentrating on the client's problem, rather than your own feelings.

You accomplish this by:

— taking notes while the person is talking;
— using paraphrasing to be sure that you understand the person's problem. This proves that you have been listening to what he or she is saying;
— asking questions.

Passing the buck, saying you're not responsible or defending your company is not the answer. The customer doesn't care whether the mistake is yours or someone else's; he or she just wants you to remove the problem. You'll stay calmer if you don't take a defensive stance. Usually, when you've solved the problem, the client will say, "I'm sorry I yelled at you!"

DO YOUR MOODS CONTROL YOU?

Before you can tackle difficult people, it's essential that you have your own act together. Could your actions or behaviour contribute to the other person's difficult behaviour?

Too often, we let others control how we feel about ourselves. We allow them to give us bad or good days. My life changed when I realized that I could choose how I reacted when confronted with difficult situations. I could either take the bad feelings being handed to me by others or simply not take them. When I learned this simple technique, I found I had far more control over my everyday moods. Gone were the roller-coaster mood swings of the past. Other people didn't decide what kind of day I'd have — I did! You, too, can have this control. Mind you, there will be exceptions to this, but many moods and reactions you *can* control. If you control the little difficulties, you're better equipped to handle the really big ones.

Picture this scene: You're driving to work, feeling pretty good about yourself and life. Suddenly, a car swerves in front of you, nearly causing a collision. You slam on the brakes (everything on the front seat goes flying) and hope for the best. Your car stops inches from the offending car. You peel yourself off the steering wheel, scrunch over to pick things up off the floor and look for the car that cut you off. It has disappeared.

What's your first reaction — to rant and rave about rotten drivers? How long do you stay mad at the driver of the other car? And what good does it do? I've seen people stay at a fever pitch for hours, relating their experience to anyone who will listen.

When the car cut you off, you had two choices. You could stay upset about it, or admit you were in an emergency situation that you handled well, and continue calmly driving to work.

If you *chose* to remain upset, you can't blame the other driver for it. What you do after something negative happens to you is *your* decision, not the other person's. If you allow someone else to upset you, you've made the wrong choice.

Here's another example. You've worked very hard completing an assignment and are very proud of your accomplishment. You wait . . . and *wait* for some kind of recognition from your supervisor. Is it likely to come? In many instances — no. You're more likely to hear about the small portion of the assignment you did wrong.

In addition to this, you're probably your own worst critic. There's a little twerp in all of us who is forever criticizing us. It says such things as, "Well, you goofed again! Can't you do anything right?"

Learn to stop criticizing yourself and start giving yourself positive reinforcement. If you've done a good job, you should mentally pat yourself on the back with such thoughts as, "I'm really proud of how I did that job." Don't count on others to do this. If they do, think of their praise as "gravy" — but you don't need gravy on the potatoes every night, do you? Like too much gravy (which can make you swell up), too much praise can make you swell-headed. The person you should be trying to please is yourself. Never compete against the record of someone else. Just improve your own record of accomplishments.

The next time something like this happens to you, don't accept the negative feelings it causes. This takes hard, concentrated effort on your part. Practise this skill until you automatically respond the way you want to. You may find yourself slipping back into your old defensive or retaliatory ways, but keep at it. If you do, you'll be able to keep your cool more often when under fire.

Whenever you're having any strong negative feeling, stop to evaluate whether the feeling is realistic or not. These feelings include guilt, frustration, defencelessness, anger, hurt, desire for revenge, anxiety, jealousy, envy, defeatedness, defensiveness, weakness, depression or dependence. If you've determined that the feeling is not realistic, don't let the words or actions of the other person affect you. Ask yourself whether you're overreacting, or reacting with the correct emotion to the situation. By doing this, you stay in charge of your emotions, and therefore maintain control over the situation.

Do you have mood swings that affect what kind of day you have? Are you up one day, down the next — up one hour, down the next? Many times this depends on what's happening around you — somebody snarls at you or gives you a mountainous job to do. You think, "Oh God, give me strength!" It's the little annoyances that can ruin your day, so if you can handle them constructively, you're certainly ahead of the game.

The Positive Approach
I'm sure there have been times when you've had a day where everything's gone wrong. You wish you could go back to bed (and it's only 10:00 a.m.). How you react to this kind of day often determines its outcome. Most people respond by saying, "Oh boy. It's going to be one of those days!" They expect the rest of the day to be as bad — and, of course, it is!

After three or four things have gone wrong in a day, have a talk with yourself. Instead of saying, "It's going to be one of those days," say, "Thank goodness I got *that* over with." What you're doing is telling yourself that the rest of the day is going to be better. Try changing to a positive attitude when you're having a bad day and see if it doesn't turn things around.

Ways People Deal with Negative Feelings
Many people believe (incorrectly) that bad emotions are always dangerous and powerful. If they express these feelings openly, they tell themselves, they'll lose someone's love or provoke people's anger, boredom or dislike. They can't accept, either, that wanting to be liked by everybody all the time is an unrealistic goal.

Other people believe (also incorrectly) that it's "unhealthy" or "dishonest" to try to control how they express their feelings. They believe they have the right to let people know how they feel in any manner they choose, no matter what the circumstances – or the consequences.

Most people believe there are only two things they can do with bad emotions: (a) repress them or (b) express them in the form in which they experience them – that is, negatively. Most of us are also aware that both ways can be pretty destructive.

a) Repression

Some people are out of touch with their emotions and lack insight into their own bad moods. These are often people who are so afraid of the power of their emotions that they can't admit to having them (denial). Others are all too aware of how they feel but can't think of a constructive way of expressing their feelings, so force themselves to suppress the outward signs.

If you are one of these people, you may realize that such methods spare others but hurt you. If you don't deal with the feelings, they don't go away. Instead they show themselves as some of the following symptoms:

Depression.   This can result from bad feelings that people turn against themselves because they feel helpless to do anything about a problem. The resulting depression can become severe.

Psychosomatic illnesses.   Repression of bad feelings can cause many physical illnesses. Some of these are tension headaches, stiff muscles, insomnia, eating disorders, migraine headaches, ulcers and heart attacks.

Low self-esteem.   One of the more pathetic results of repression is a tendency to turn bad feelings inward upon the self. Instead of venting their anger against the blocking conditions, such people attack themselves and wind up feeling, "I'm no good."

Emotional withdrawal.   People who react this way become apathetic, indifferent, uninvolved. They give the impression of just going through the motions.

Recourse to drugs or alcohol.   Repressed emotions can also lead people to seek escape or release through substance abuse.

b) Destructive Expression

The pitfalls are different for people who feel able to express negative emotions. Certain ways of openly expressing bad feelings can also be destructive, hurting the recipients and alienating people. Moody people thus may become isolated from others. Some ways of expressing bad feelings that have generally destructive effects are:

Temper tantrums. These are childish, inappropriate, uncontrolled expressions of anger that can be triggered by anything — some trivial current happening or something that took place long ago that the person has stewed about for years. People who are prone to temper tantrums may deal with the minor irritations of day-to-day life by saying nothing at the time, then, when a chance remark acts as a trigger, erupting in a red flash of rage and lashing out at the nearest person. This fury has unfortunate consequences; the person feels terrible and others are alienated.

Sulking. Sulkers are ready to show they're in a bad mood but refuse to explain why. The "silent treatment" and "acting hurt" are variants of sulking.

Sarcasm. People who resort to sarcasm to express negative emotions are usually reluctant to confront the cause of their bad mood directly.

Logic Versus Emotion: The Analytical Approach

If negative emotions go in, they have to get out somehow. We have seen some of the instinctive ways people deal with them. Most of these instinctive and/or impulsive reactions have negative consequences. The challenge is to find ways to deal with negative emotions constructively.

Two forces — logic and emotion — are at work throughout our lives. Often they push and pull in opposite directions. The one that prevails at any particular time will determine how we get along with others and may affect our level of achievement. It's easy to respond to situations with emotions rather than logic, but responding logically helps us deal constructively with difficult circumstances.

If it does not come naturally to you to behave logically when under stress, don't be discouraged. The ability to use logic to help resolve conflicts and problems can be developed. The first step is to gain some insight into the nature of the difficulty. You can do this by analysing the situation, your feelings and your behaviour. Armed with information from this analysis, you can then learn to take charge of your reactions instead of letting your instincts control you.

Here are two examples that show how the analytical approach could be useful.

1. Suppose you feel depressed for no other reason than because it's Monday morning. Do you phone in sick, or do you try to figure out what's wrong? When you analyse your reactions, you realize that you regularly have an upper on Friday afternoon and a downer on Monday morning. You may be one of the more than 80 per cent of employed people who are in the wrong job. Do you let that depress you further, or do you do the logical thing and seriously consider looking for more suitable employment?

When you consider that most of us spend ten hours a day, five days a week either getting ready for, travelling to or in the work place, it's a shame that people don't spend more energy deciding what they would like to do with their lives. If you find yourself in the wrong job or occupation and decide to look for something you enjoy more, you could start by contacting one of the career agencies listed in the Appendix.

2. Or suppose you are under pressure to finish a job by 2:00 p.m., when your supervisor suddenly gives you an extra batch of work. Because your supervisor often does this, you find that you regularly have difficulty completing your allotted work on time. This makes you feel inadequate. On the other hand, you don't want to annoy your supervisor by saying no. Do you try to avoid saying no to your supervisor and end up at 2:00 p.m. having to say, "I'm sorry, boss, I haven't finished it yet"? Or do you say, "I won't have time to complete both this and the Jones report by 2:00 p.m. Which would you rather I do?"

In the first case, your supervisor is angry with you anyway because, by not speaking up, you prevented her from making other arrangements for completing the report. You then complain, saying, "My job makes me feel that I'm under a lot of pressure."

In the second case, your analysis of such situations has made you realize that it is your supervisor's responsibility to help you set priorities. To ensure she can do this effectively, you make sure you have a good idea of your present work load. Perhaps you have taken a time-management course to help you choose priorities. You keep "To do" lists, so you know exactly how much you can handle in a day, and you are careful to keep your supervisor informed of your work load.

Analysing Stress

Certain physical and behavioural symptoms are associated with stress. Physical signs may include tense muscles, gritted teeth or clenched jaw, rapid pulse, pounding heart, increased perspiration, shortness of breath, a rise in blood pressure, clammy skin, cold hands and feet, sluggish digestion, rapid breathing, heightened sensitivity to noise and "racing" thoughts. Stress-related behaviour may include impatience, restlessness, sudden rages or bouts of laughing or weeping and a tendency to heightened emotion of all types. In some cases depression and apathy may also be reactions to stress.

Not all stress is bad. The heightened emotions and physical symptoms associated with stress can occur in response to pleasurable and exciting events — such as being promoted or falling in love. It's not stress in itself that's the problem, then, but negative stress — the kind that produces *distress*.

For example, most people assume that workaholics are unhappy, but that's not always true. There are two basic kinds of workaholic. There are those who love their jobs and work hard and long because they receive pleasure from doing so. They're under stress but seldom suffer from real *distress*.

Other workaholics are motivated not by enthusiasm but by such things as:

— competitive feelings;
— job pressures;
— budget cuts;
— family or relationship problems;
— financial problems.

Their stress becomes *distress* and they suffer because of it. We all know these people; they:

— work all the time, often bringing work home in the evening and on the weekend — but are resentful about it;
— suffer from nervous disorders;
— don't eat or exercise right;
— never take time off from work when they're ill. (They're the

ones who pass on the flu bug to the rest of the staff because they come in when they shouldn't.);
— seldom spend time with their family;
— don't know how to relax, or play or simply "have fun." (They often use competitive sports to relax.)

If you suspect you're a workaholic, the following questionnaire may give you further insight into whether your work is a source of positive or negative stress:

Are You a Workaholic?

Part A

		Yes	No
1.	Are you always punctual for appointments?		
2.	Are you more comfortable when you're productive than idle?		
3.	Do you carefully organize your hobbies?		
4.	When you participate in recreational activities, is it mainly with work associates?		
5.	Even under pressure, do you usually take the extra time to make sure you have all the facts before you make a decision?		
6.	Are most of your friends in the same line of work as you?		
7.	Is most of your reading work-related?		
8.	Do you work late more frequently than your peers?		
9.	Do you talk shop over coffee or cocktails on social occasions?		
10.	Do your dreams centre on work- or family-related conflicts?		
11.	Do you play as hard as you work?		
12.	Do you become restless on holiday?		
13.	Do your spouse and friends think of you as an easygoing person?		

If you answered yes to the first twelve questions and no to question 13, you're a workaholic, all right; but keep in mind that this is not bad unless it's causing you *dis*tress. To find out if your workaholism is a source of negative stress, answer the questions in Part B.

Part B

	Yoo	No
14. Do you seem to communicate better with your co-workers than with your spouse (or best friend)?	_____	_____
15. Are you better able to relax on Saturdays than on Sunday afternoons?	_____	_____
16. Do you take work to bed with you when you're home sick?	_____	_____
17. Are you usually very annoyed when others keep you waiting?	_____	_____
18. Do you wake up in the night worrying about business or family problems?	_____	_____
19. In competitive sports do you occasionally see your supervisor's face on the ball?	_____	_____
20. Is work sometimes a way of avoiding close relationships?	_____	_____
21. Do you usually plan every step of the itinerary of a trip in advance and become uncomfortable if plans go awry?	_____	_____
22. Do you enjoy small talk at a cocktail party or reception?	_____	_____

If you answered yes to questions 14 through 21 and no to question 22, you're probably not enjoying your long, hard hours of work.

If your *distress* keeps up long enough, the almost inevitable result will be *burnout*. To check for signs of burnout, ask yourself the following questions.

Do I:

— feel down or depressed most of the time?
— feel tired most of the time?
— have trouble eating and sleeping properly?
— feel there's no hope for improvement in my circumstances?
— complain constantly?
— feel that no one cares?
— feel upset, frustrated or angry most of the time?
— experience feelings of intense pressure and competition at work?

— feel that, no matter what I do, it won't be enough?
— fear that I'm going under any day now?

The first step in dealing with *dis*tress is to analyse all the sources of stress in your life to determine, first, which are positive and which are negative, and second, which you can do something about and which you can't change. To do this, go through the following exercise as accurately as you can. Write down your answers, don't just go through the exercise mentally.

1. On a sheet of paper, list everything that's causing you stress. (Leave space between each stressor.) Try to give at least five stressors.
2. On a scale of 1 to 10 (10 being the highest) determine the stress level of each stressor.
3. Determine if the stressor is positive (a wedding, a promotion, a new baby, a new job) or negative (rudeness, driving in rush-hour traffic).
4. Put down the feelings you have when in the stressful situation (anger, frustration, happiness, fear) next to each stressor.
5. Identify which part of your life is most affected by each negative stressor (family, social, business/work).
6. Then for each negative stressor determine whether:
   a. you *do* have the power to alleviate the problem. Put the word "do" next to the item; or
   b. you *don't* have the power to change the situation. It's beyond your control — there's nothing you can do about it. Put the word "don't" next to the item.

Techniques for Reducing Negative Stress
Once you have identified the negative sources of stress in your life and have determined which of them you could do something about, you're well on the way to obtaining relief from the worst pressures.

Your analysis should then be followed by two more steps:

7. If you don't have the power to do something about a negative source of stress, forget about it. Mentally throw the problem in the garbage can and don't waste any more precious energy thinking about it.

8. If you do have the power to change the situation, think about what you are going to do about it. Draw up a plan of action.

These steps put the Serenity Prayer (written by Reinhold Niebuhr) into practice:
"God grant me the serenity to accept the things I cannot change, the courage to change the things I can, and the wisdom to know the difference."

One of my seminar participants identified the following problem: "My personal annoyance is rush-hour traffic. Almost every day, I get into a bad mood watching the dumb things other drivers do."

This is probably one of the things in your life that you have no control over. What you do have control over is your reaction to it. Drive defensively. Remind yourself not to get upset. Use your energy constructively, by tuning in to your favourite radio station or playing a tape you enjoy. You might consider travelling earlier or later to miss traffic jams.

I have a very busy and stressful life and find that every once in a while things start piling up on me. I've found that the step-by-step process just identified works well for me. Completed once or twice a year (or whenever necessary), it reduces my stress level by half and sometimes more.

When I get to step six, I can normally throw out one-third of the things I've been worrying about, put some on "hold," and concentrate on changing the situations I *do* have control over. I can channel my energies in the right direction, choosing a course of action that cuts out much of my worry, frustration and anger.

Analysing Anger
One of the most common negative emotions people feel is anger. Many emotions, such as fear, anxiety or guilt, do not start out as anger but may be expressed as anger. And many signs of illness, depression and unhappiness can be caused by anger that is being suppressed.

The analytical approach can give you a head start in dealing with your own and other people's anger. It can help you discover the cause of the anger and identify strategies for dealing with it that are or are not working.

Certain situations may be more likely than others to make you angry. Or you may be able to express anger more readily in some circumstances than others. The list that follows is not exhaustive. It's just a guide to the kinds of questions you could ask yourself to gain insight into your anger.

I get angry most frequently:

— *at work.*   If so, break it down. Does your anger have to do with co-workers, subordinates, superiors?
— *in impersonal situations.*   Some people can only show their anger to taxi drivers and others who can't retaliate.
— *with friends and acquaintances.*   With some people, the more distant the acquaintance is, the easier they find it to express anger. With others it's the reverse. The closer the friend, the easier it is to say, "I'm furious."
— *in social situations.*   Can you get angry in a group conversation but not one on one, or vice versa? You may feel safer in a group — or the opposite.
— *in close relationships.*   Some can express anger only to a spouse. When asked why, the answer is often: "He or she is the only person in the world who won't reject me if I show anger."
— *at a particular time.*   Do you become angry more often at night? In the morning? On a particular day of the week, or during one season of the year? Check to see if some event or set of responsibilities is associated with that particular time.

Once you have some insight into the times and places you are most likely to feel angry and the situations in which you are or are not able to express your feelings, you're ready to explore the ways in which you deal with your own and others' anger. Again, the list is not exhaustive. If your own behaviour isn't mentioned here, add it to the list.

Dealing With Anger
Circle the best answer.
My Own Anger
1. When I'm angry, I usually feel:
   a. afraid to say anything directly, because I don't want to hurt the other person's feelings.

   b. afraid that if I do say something, it will sound aggressive and others won't like me.

   c. okay about expressing what's on my mind.

   d. anxious and confused about what I want to say.

2. When I'm angry with someone, I usually:

   a. keep quiet.

   b. drop hints about my feelings, hoping he or she will get the message.

   c. tell the person in a direct way what I want, and feel okay about it.

   d. avoid the other person for a while, while I calm down and the anger wears off.

   e. blow up and tell him or her off.

   f. simmer for days, then vent my anger in a big blow-up.

   g. express my anger sarcastically, getting my point across with some humour or a dig.

   h. take out my anger on someone other than the person at whom I'm angry.

   i. act hurt instead of angry.

   j. label the other person, rather than trying to deal with his or her behaviour.

Other People's Anger

3. When someone gets angry with me, I usually feel:

   a. that he or she doesn't like me.

   b. too scared to ask why.

   c. confused and upset.

   d. that I have a right to understand why he or she is angry and to respond to it.

   e. hurt or wronged.

   f. guilty.

4. When someone gets angry with me, I usually:

   a. lose my cool and end up blustering.

   b. back off.

   c. ask him or her to explain further, or respond in some other equally straightforward manner.

   d. get angry in return (retaliate verbally).

   e. apologize, even if I don't understand why he or she is angry.

   f. make a joke out of it, and try to get him or her to forget the flare-up.

   g. give him or her the "silent treatment."

Rate Yourself

The following answers identify constructive beliefs and behaviour:

1. c 2. c and d 3. d 4. c

Techniques for Dealing with Anger

Constructive beliefs and behaviour are those that allow you to respect your own rights and the rights of others while taking action to remove the cause of the anger. What do you do if your analysis revealed that (a) you can't express anger when you need to? or that (b) you react to your own and others' anger in unconstructive ways?

For the first problem — (a) — you need to practise some basic self-psychology.

- *Recognize that you have a right to feel anger and express it.*
  Anger doesn't have to lead to violence or more anger. Your goal is to learn to deal with anger constructively, not to ignore it or repress it.

- *Don't rationalize your reluctance to express anger.*
  Excuses like "I won't say anything because I'll hurt the other person's feelings" are ways of explaining to yourself why you don't do what you've never learned to do. Instead of dwelling on the reasons why you don't express anger, concentrate on learning how to do it.

For the second problem — (b) — you need information about the constructive alternatives available to you and practice in using some of them.

- *Remember that your choice is not limited to expressing anger or not expressing it.*
  Sometimes you can use a supportive approach. For example, your supervisor yells at you and orders you to do something you consider completely unprofessional. Count to ten, and say, "Is there something wrong, Mr. Bailey? I know there must be, or you would never speak to me that way."

- *When appropriate, make the deliberate decision not to express anger.*
  Initially, expressing anger may make you feel important. There are times though, when you cannot express your anger. For example, when a frail older person angers you, your angry response may endanger his or her health.

- If your anger brings about tension and interferes with things you do, get it out of your system with physical exercise (*not* competitive sports!). This works when you're not able to express anger — for instance, if the other person is out of town.

- In your bedroom, hit your pillow for two minutes, curse into the pillow. Release your anger in some harmless physical way.
- Share your feelings with the person who upset you. Communicate: don't shut him or her out.
- Be forthright about your anger and follow through. Some people make tentative stabs at expression of anger, then give up. Don't just mention that you're angry and let it drop; work at finding a solution to the problem or situation that caused the anger.
- If you have trouble venting your anger to someone close to you, write down all the things that make you furious with that person. Ask him or her to do the same and regularly make appointments to get together. Don't dump on each other; just discuss the important items on your respective lists. Make a vow to each other that you will listen and try to understand the other person's position. Take turns: one talks, the other listens, without interrupting.
- Focus on the *behaviour* of the person causing the anger. Don't attack the person; the person's *actions* are what should concern you.
- Determine ways you could have handled your anger better than you did at the time it occurred and rehearse the alternatives with someone you trust.

STYLES OF BEHAVIOUR AND THEIR EFFECTS

To a large extent your ability to deal *constructively* with stress, anger and difficult situations depends on the *style of behaviour* you most readily adopt.

Are you passive or socially compliant — sacrificing your own needs and becoming a doormat? Are you aggressive — satisfying your own needs and hurting others? Or are you nicely assertive — with realistic concern for yourself but also concern for the needs and feelings of those around you? To determine which of these behaviour styles most closely resembles your own, think about how you would respond in the following case:

You have one hour in which to go to the bank and eat your lunch. You get to the bank and find that everyone else in the city seems to be there. As you finally approach the head of the line, someone stops to chat with the person in front of you and makes moves to ease into the line before you.

You:

a. say nothing.
b. let her stay, muttering about people who butt into line.
c. ask her to go to the back of the line, explaining that you've been waiting a long time.
d. bawl her out and tell her to go to the end of the line.
e. make a sarcastic remark about her behaviour.

Which did you choose? The most constructive response is c. What kind of behaviour was being displayed by the person butting in? Right — aggressive. Would you have felt that you were acting aggressively yourself if you did c? You shouldn't, because what you were doing was (correctly) standing up for your rights.

The behaviours described in examples a through e are, in order:

a. Passive behaviour.
b. Passive resistant behaviour.
c. Assertive behaviour.
d. Aggressive behaviour.
e. Indirect aggressive behaviour.

There are three basic behaviour types.

1. *Passive behaviour* characterizes people who seldom if ever express their own wants and needs. Instead, they give in to the demands and wants of others. They're reluctant to defend their rights or to stand up for themselves. Their behaviour shows that they don't respect themselves. For example:

Marge: Where do you want to go for lunch today? Should we go to Roberto's [Italian food] or to The Wok [Chinese food]?
Sally: I don't care. [She likes Chinese food.]
Marge: I feel like spaghetti — so let's go to Roberto's!
Sally: Okay, if you want to.

Sally acted passively and didn't let Marge know where she wanted to go. Marge is expected to guess. This seldom happens, so Sally remains silent and Marge gets her way.

2. *Aggressive behaviour* characterizes people who show little respect for the needs and wants of others. Everything must go their way. They lack empathy and have difficulty placing themselves in others' shoes. They take advantage of others, especially when others show weakness. That's when they pounce and go in for the kill. For example:

Betty: Sandy, can you give me a ride home tonight?
Sandy: I can't. I have to go grocery shopping after work.
Betty: That's okay. I have to pick up some groceries too.
Sandy: I'd rather not, tonight.
Betty: How come?
Sandy: It's just not convenient for me — I'll be rushed as it is.
Betty: I'd do it for you! Some friend you are!

Betty had the right to ask Sandy for a ride, but when she tried to force her wishes and desires on Sandy, her behaviour became aggressive. Betty forced Sandy to defend herself and attempted to give Sandy a guilt trip when she wouldn't comply with her wishes.

Passive resistance and indirect aggression are variants of these two basic types of behaviour.

Passive resistance is often used by passive people who are trying to become more assertive in their behaviour. They mutter and sigh a lot and play manipulative games to get their way. They've not learned to ask, up front, for what they want. For example:

Joe: Bob, can you drive me to work today?

Bob had his morning planned and it would be inconvenient for him to do so. Joe had been asking this question several times in the past week because his car signal lights weren't working. Joe hadn't made much effort to correct the problem.

Bob: Joe, I've driven you twice this week . . .
Joe: Can you make an exception this time?
Bob: (letting out a big sigh): Oh, all right!

Bob's body language and way of giving in imply an unstated criticism: "Just look at the sacrifices I make for you. If you looked after your car better this wouldn't have happened!" He doesn't have the courage to state his objections directly.

Indirect aggression is used by people who want to express hostility without suffering the retaliation that direct aggression often invites. They use subtle, underhanded methods to get their way, such as sabotage, sarcasm, the silent treatment and gossip. All these tactics are very destructive to both parties. For example:

Don: My boss gave me a rotten assignment that he expects me to have ready by four o'clock. I'm going to leave out some important information so he won't give me another job like that in the future. [Sabotage.]

Bill: Oh sure, Mark's really smart . . . he got 40 per cent on the last test in his marketing course! [Sarcasm.]

Linda hadn't spoken to her co-worker Anne-Louise for four days after an argument. They hadn't resolved the issue, even though Anne-Louise had tried several times to get her to talk about the problem. [Silent treatment.]

Jill: Did you hear about Carmen's husband? He was picked up for drunk driving last night. [Gossip.]

3. *Assertive behaviour* characterizes people who respect both themselves and others. They're comfortable expressing their needs to others and defending their rights when necessary. They recognize that others have needs and rights as well. Assertive people are good negotiators. They don't expect to win all the time and are willing to give in if the issue is important to another person. For example:

Marge: Where do you want to go for lunch today? Should we go to Roberto's [Italian food] or to The Wok [Chinese food]?

Sally: I prefer The Wok. How about you?

Marge: My mouth is watering for some spaghetti.

Sally: I don't mind having that today. Let's go there.

Marge: Let's make plans to go to The Wok next Tuesday, okay?

Sally: Sure, it sounds good to me!

Try to use assertive behaviour most of the time. Nobody can force you to give up your rights. The only person who can give up those rights is you, the person who owns them. You become less of a person if you give up your rights to another person unless you have determined it's best for both parties.

Behaviour Styles and Traditional Roles

Women
Many women still follow the behaviour of their mothers and grandmothers. They believe that passive behaviour is appropriate for women and that women who compete or become too powerful are unfeminine.

Women who succeed in business have had to unlearn this traditional behaviour and become more assertive. Some, however, in their attempts to change, have gone to the other extreme and have become aggressive.

Men
Many men, on the other hand, retain the traditional belief that their role in life is to be strong, competitive and aggressive. To adapt to new thinking and circumstances in business, men are having to change. They're acting less aggressively and are becoming more in tune with their feelings and the feelings of others.

How Passive People Feel About Themselves

People who normally use passive behaviour likely feel:

- Angry — They *know* others take advantage of them.
- Frustrated — They seldom get their way.
- Withdrawn — They believe nobody listens to them.
- Insecure and inferior — They lack self-esteem and self-confidence, are unaware of their abilities, and are reluctant to try new things for fear of failing.
- Anxious — They feel they have little control over their lives.
- Defeated — They believe it's no use trying; they won't get what they want anyway.
- Unable to acknowledge feelings — They hide feelings of fear and inadequacy by pretending everything's all right.

- Liable to put themselves down — have difficulty accepting even the simplest compliment and tend to underestimate the value of what they do.
- Lacking in energy – Their zest for living is missing. They're usually doing things that others want them to do, rather than what *they* themselves want.

These people believe they're not okay, but you are okay.

How Aggressive People Feel About Themselves

People who normally use aggressive behaviour likely feel:

- Powerful (in the short run) — They enjoy having people scurry and rush to do what they say.
- Guilty (eventually) — They know they're taking advantage of others.
- Threatened — They constantly let others know how good, intelligent, strong, etc., they are. They do this because others may learn they aren't really that good underneath their veneer. They attempt to make themselves feel important by putting others down.
- Right — They are convinced that the only ideas worth listening to are their own.
- Critical — They blame others when things go wrong.
- Lonely — Their aggression isolates them from everyone around them.
- Excessively energetic — They expend energy in the wrong direction, doing destructive rather than constructive things.

These people feel that they're okay, but you're not okay. Those who hit the outer edge of aggressive behaviour (criminals) believe that they're not okay, but you're not okay either.

How Assertive People Feel About Themselves

People who normally use assertive behaviour likely feel:

- Positive — They approach every new task or idea with a positive rather than a negative attitude.

- Calm — They're at peace with themselves and others.
- Enthusiastic — They complete tasks with zest and feel that they'll succeed at them.
- Proud — They accomplish what they do without stealing ideas from others or climbing over others. They can take full credit for what they achieve.
- Honest — When they give their word that they'll do something, they do it, so others believe in them.
- Direct — They don't play manipulative games to get what they want. They are up front in situations, and usually succeed at what they attempt.
- Confident — They take risks, but know their limitations. They know that it's okay to be wrong sometimes and are ready to learn from their mistakes.
- Satisfied — They know where they're going and how they're going to get there, so they usually attain their goals.
- In control — They seldom have mood swings that adversely affect their communication with and behaviour towards others.
- Able to acknowledge feelings — They can explain to others what unpleasant behaviour is doing to them.
- Respect for others — They recognize that others have needs and rights just as they do.
- Energetic — Their energy is directed towards achieving their goals.

These people feel that they're okay, and you're okay too.

Consequences of These Behavioural Styles

It's helpful to know how others are likely to react to you when you use different behavioural styles.

Passive Behaviour

Passive behaviour can make others feel aggressive. People may shun someone who gives in again and again to their wishes. They don't like the guilty feelings they have when passive people allow themselves to be taken advantage of.

For example, Sarah was responsible for ensuring that the

receptionist in the office (Judy) had someone to take over her duties during coffee, lunch and bathroom breaks. There were four employees on the list that Sarah could call on for this duty. Several of them were sick or couldn't spare the time one week, so Mary had to cover for Judy all that week. This made Mary get behind in her own work, and she had to work overtime two days that week.

The same problem existed the next two weeks, and Sarah had to rely on Mary again. Mary willingly worked the second week. Sarah felt terrible asking her to cover the post the third week, but grudgingly, Mary again agreed.

From then on, every time Sarah saw Mary she felt guilty. She realized that, although she was normally an assertive person, she felt as though she had taken advantage of Mary (had acted aggressively) — she felt guilty. To combat this guilty feeling she avoided Mary and didn't have normal contact with her.

Mary helped Sarah out because she wanted Sarah to like her, but ended up with a negative reaction (exactly what she tried not to do). Many passive people have this unexpected reaction to their "good deeds" and wonder what they've done wrong or how they may have offended others.

Dealing with passive people can also make others feel:

- Irritated — They wish you'd stand up for yourself and make your own decisions.
- Withdrawn — They avoid you because your negative attitude makes it difficult for them to maintain their own positive attitude.
- Superior — They lose respect for you as a person, because you aren't willing to stand up for what you believe in.
- Tired — They waste valuable energy dealing with their negative reactions to you.

Aggressive Behaviour

Aggressive behaviour can make others feel:

- Angry and threatened — They resent your unfair tactics.
- Frustrated — They waste valuable energy defending themselves from your abusive ways.
- Withdrawn — They avoid you because when you're around, they feel they must be ready to defend themselves.

- Anxious and defensive — They can't relax because they're preparing for the next attack.
- Resentful — They resent the power you seem to have over them.
- Hurt — They can't help being affected by your put-downs, even if they know your comments are undeserved.
- Humiliated — They don't enjoy being corrected or made to appear foolish in public.
- Tired — They waste valuable energy preparing for what you're going to throw at them next.

Assertive Behaviour
Assertive behaviour can make others feel:

- Positive — They sense that you will be pleased if they succeed.
- Secure — They trust you, because you let them know where they stand with you by offering constant feedback.
- Co-operative — They respond to your straightforward positive behaviour by trying to help you.
- Respectful — They reciprocate the respect you show for their needs and rights.
- Energetic — They're able to use their energy constructively because there's no game-playing.

Who Wins?

Do assertive people usually achieve their goals? Yes, because their aim is for both sides to win. They believe in equality and are willing to negotiate.

Do passive people usually achieve their goals? No, because they seldom have goals in the first place. They expect others to look after them.

Do aggressive people usually achieve their goals? Sometimes, in the short run, but they often face antagonism and retaliation later.

Analysing Blocks to Assertiveness

Your answers to the following questions can help you to identify areas where you have difficulty asserting yourself.

Dealing with People in Authority

1. When I need something from a busy professional, I feel that:
   a. I'm important too, so I should receive immediate attention.
   b. I should apologize for taking up his or her time.
   c. I shouldn't call until I absolutely have to.
   d. I should state directly what I need and ask for what I want.
2. When I need something from a busy professional, I think he or she will:
   a. make me feel inferior.
   b. be pleased that I'm interested.
   c. resent my taking up valuable time.

Saying No to Others' Requests

3. If someone wants a favour and I don't want to do it, I usually:
   a. apologize profusely and tell him or her I'd rather not do it.
   b. do it anyway.
   c. tell him or her I'd rather not do it.
   d. make excuses about why I can't do it.
   e. tell him or her I resent the request, but do it grudgingly.
4. If I refuse to do someone a favour, I think he or she will:
   a. act as though he or she doesn't mind, but secretly resent me.
   b. hate me.
   c. think I don't like him or her.
   d. be angry with me.
   e. understand and not mind.
   f. hesitate to ask me again.

Making Requests of Others

5. When I need someone to do something for me, I usually:
   a. apologetically explain why I need help.
   b. ask directly for what I want, knowing that he or she has the right to refuse my request.
   c. ask only if I'm absolutely desperate.
   d. insist on getting my way.
   e. do nice things for the person, hoping he or she will return the favour.
6. When I need someone to do something for me, I usually feel:
   a. afraid to ask, because he or she might say no.
   b. that I'm bothering the person or putting him or her on the spot.
   c. that it's all right to ask. The person can say no.
   d. that he or she should do what I want.

Communicating
7. At business socials where I don't know anyone I usually:
    a. rush for food, a drink or a cigarette to make it look as if I'm having a good time.
    b. introduce myself to someone who looks interesting.
    c. wait for someone to talk to me.
    d. keep to myself by staying on the sidelines.
    e. put a lampshade on my head or use other attention-getting actions.
8. At a social where I don't know anyone, I usually:
    a. think of ways to get attention.
    b. worry that I won't be able to say the right thing if someone talks to me.
    c. look forward to meeting new people.
    d. worry that no one will talk to me.
    e. think that everyone seems relaxed except me.
    f. feel that I'm out of place, and everyone knows it.

Rate Yourself. The following show assertive attitudes or actions:
1. d 2. b 3. c 4. e 5. b 6. c 7. b 8. c

If you didn't do well, don't worry — nobody's perfect. Look over your answers. On questions where your responses matched the assertive responses identified, you're good at asserting yourself. On questions where your responses did not match the assertive responses, try to identify specific situations in your life that fit those problem categories. Look at the questions again and try to figure out just what irrational beliefs may be blocking your assertiveness.

APPROACHES TO CONFLICT RESOLUTION
We have seen that many conflicts and resentments arise because people feel either that they have to defend themselves against an aggressor or that they have inadvertently taken advantage of a too-passive person. The ability to behave assertively rather than aggressively or passively can significantly reduce the level of conflict and stress in your life; however, conflicts cannot be avoided entirely. When they do arise, the principles of assertive behaviour that are so effective for preventing conflicts are also helpful for resolving them.

The basic approaches to resolving conflicts are:

1. *Competition.*   One person or group wins, the other loses.
2. *Accommodation.*   One person refuses even to state his or her wishes, but simply goes along with the other's statements or demands.
3. *Compromise/Collaboration.*   Each person recognizes the other's rights. Each may need to yield on some points, but it is understood that the solution must take into account the needs and wishes of both.

There are no competitive feelings in the last approach. Instead, there is a feeling of co-operation or camaraderie among the participants. This attitude uses each person's talents and recognizes each person's rights.

You are now equipped with some basic insights into human behaviour — your own and that of others. You will be able to switch off your defense mechanism when faced with negative comments and actions from others. The tool that will allow you to make effective use of these insights is your ability to communicate well with the people you encounter. In the next two chapters, you will learn the specific communication skills you will need for dealing with difficult people.

CHAPTER
TWO

BASIC COMMUNICATION SKILLS

There are many skills that will help you deal with difficult people. If you find that you're often misunderstood, or that you misunderstand others too often, the following skill is a must for you to practise and use.

PARAPHRASING

Paraphrasing means: to express meaning in other words; to rephrase; to give a message in another form; to amplify a message.

We normally use paraphrasing for simple things such as repeating telephone numbers when taking a message.

The use of paraphrasing is essential when two people are conversing at any time. Unfortunately, when information isn't clear to us, we often make assumptions. We don't confirm with other people that what we *thought* they said was what they really meant us to understand.

You are receiving instructions on how to get to someone's house. You neglected to use paraphrasing to confirm that you have understood the directions, and you end up completely lost. Sound familiar?

Here's an example of two people talking but not understanding each other:

Bill: Jim didn't get that job he wanted.
Jennie: He didn't get the job he wanted?
Bill: Yeah, and he's really upset about it.

In this conversation, Jennie thought she was using paraphrasing, but all she was doing was parroting what Bill said. Instead, she should have asked herself what Bill's statement *meant* to her. Some of her assumptions could have been:

— Jim asked for too much money.
— He was overqualified for the position.
— He was underqualified for the position.
— He blew the interview.
— Someone else was better than he.
— He's probably better suited to a different career.

If she had determined what the statement meant to her (Jim blew the interview) and had used paraphrasing, the earlier conversation would have been more like this:

Bill: Jim didn't get that job he wanted.
Jennie: You mean he blew the interview?
Bill: Oh no, he learned that they had already chosen someone else for the position before he applied.
Jennie: I'm sorry to hear that.
Bill: Yeah, and he's really upset about it.

You can see the difference between these two sets of conversations. In the first conversation, Bill and Jennie do not confirm their personal beliefs with each other. Bill believes that Jennie knows that Jim didn't get the job because they had someone else chosen for the position. Jennie, on the other hand, believes that Bill has confirmed her belief that Jim blew the interview. This is why problems occurred later: in a conversation with another friend, Jennie stated that both she and Bill agreed that Jim had blown the interview. She honestly believed that she was speaking the truth to her friend.

This kind of problem arises in many conversations. Ask for more information if you're not sure what a person means, or use paraphrasing to bring out discrepancies. You probably use this technique already but haven't been aware of it. If anyone has ever exclaimed, "No, that's not what I meant," you've already used paraphrasing and maybe didn't even know it! Use it often; it lessens communication problems.

It's also an excellent tool to use when clients are angry at something. If you write down details of the situation you're trying to correct, you're less likely to be spending your energy defending yourself. When the client has given all the information you need to solve the problem, use paraphrasing to make sure he or she knows you understand. The client will likely calm down and give you the opportunity to help.

Using Paraphrasing in Training Others

If you've had the responsibility of training others, you've probably had to explain more than once how to do something. Paraphrasing is a very effective tool to use when training others, especially if they're lazy listeners. To help them retain their training, do the following:

1. Give short, sequential instructions.
2. State, "To make sure that I was clear in my instructions to you, could you please explain what you're going to do?"
3. If the trainee is unable to recite the steps, repeat the instructions.
4. Again ask the trainee to recite the steps he or she will take to complete the task.

You'll find that trainees' listening skills will improve immeasurably when you use this technique. They'll know that when you train them to do anything new, there'll be a test to see if they've listened properly, and you'll find that giving instructions will be much easier in the future.

Do, however, remember that the onus is on you to make your instructions clear. Avoid such questions as:

- "Do you understand?" (People can just answer yes to this. You want to double-check by having them repeat the instructions back to you.)
- "Explain what I want you to do." (This is too overbearing. It will just put people's backs up.)
- "Did you catch that?" (This sounds like a put-down. People will resent the implication that they are stupid.)

If you think people might have misunderstood you, it's much better to make the problem yours. You can accomplish this by saying something like:

- "Let's see if I've been clear in my instructions to you."

You could then ask if they have any questions.

Those who are responsible for training others have probably thrown their hands up in the air at times. Their information seems to go in one ear and out the other with some learners. Many people require constant repetition of instructions. This type of person may be a poor listener.

Information has a better chance of being "locked in" when trainers use a variety of training methods. These could include visual aids such as movies, slides or flip charts. To help trainees further "lock in" the training, see that they use the training as soon as possible. Keep in mind that trainees retain:

— 10 per cent of what they read (handouts, manuals);
— 20 per cent of what they hear (have explained to them);
— 30 per cent of what they see done (demonstrations);
— 50 per cent of what they read, hear and see done;
— 70 per cent of what they read, hear, see done, and explain to someone else;
— 90 per cent of what they read, hear, see done, explain to someone else and do themselves.

People pass through four definite stages when learning something new. These stages are:

1. *Unconscious incompetence* — You aren't even aware that you lack the skill. For example, you may not even have known that the skill of paraphrasing existed.
2. *Conscious incompetence* — You're aware that you lack the skill. For example, before you learned how to use a computer you knew you couldn't use a computer.
3. *Conscious competence* — You know the techniques of the skill but have to stop and think before you react. ("Do I put the disk in first or turn the computer on first?")

4. *Unconscious competence* — The skill is now well established and automatic. You probably don't even think about what you're doing when you use the computer — you're on "automatic pilot."

It takes six weeks to "lock in" how to do something new; and up to three months to "lock in" doing something a different way than you used to.

These following elements are all part of the communication process:

- What I want to say/think I'm saying.
- What I actually say.
- What others think they hear.
- What others want to reply/think they're replying.
- What others actually reply.
- What I think I hear them say.

Different Interpretations of Words

Many words mean different things to different people. For example, if I invited you to my home for dinner tomorrow, when would you come? Would it be at noon or one o'clock, or at five, six, seven or eight o'clock? Some people have *dinner* (the main meal of the day) at midday, others in the evening.

If I asked people from Alaska and Florida to describe a blizzard, do you think their descriptions would be the same? Of course not — because each person has a different experience of what this word means. (And a teenager might describe a blizzard as an ice cream treat that you eat!)

Male and Female Interpretations

Often the same word has different meanings to men and women. I was with a group of people socially when a young woman in the group was discussing her career aspirations. She stated that she had attended a job interview that morning. Her boyfriend asked her whether she wanted the job.

She replied, "It will be a real challenge."

Her friend stated, "Then I guess you're not going to accept it?"

She said, "I sure will if it's offered to me! As I explained, the job's a real challenge!"

"I still don't understand why you won't be turning it down!" he repeated.

"Because it's a real challenge!" she repeated emphatically.

The conversation progressed until they ended up in a heated argument. The rest of us sat by, wondering what they were arguing about. It suddenly became apparent that they were discussing different things. To clarify matters, they were asked to explain what the word "challenge" meant to each of them.

To the woman the word "challenge" meant:

- an opportunity to stretch and reach her full potential;
- something exciting;
- an opportunity to prove herself.

To her, it was a positive word.

To her male companion, on the other hand, the word meant:

- something that prevented him from obtaining what he wanted;
- the prelude to a fight.

To him, it was a negative word.

This revelation started the group trying to identify words they felt had different meanings for men and women. We were able to come up with a few, and I'm constantly seeking others. Here are some:

Macho

To most men it meant:

- strong and decisive, a leader, a man who's given respect;
- trend-setting, a role model.

To most women (and some men) it meant:

- chauvinistic, a man who thinks he's God's gift to women;
- small-mindedness or narrow-mindedness;
- given to bullying;
- vain, a man who can't pass a mirror without stopping to check his appearance and posture.

Gentle
To most women it meant:

- tender, empathetic, in tune with others;
- reluctant to take advantage of others;
- dependable, unassuming, trustworthy, kind-hearted.

To most men it meant:

- mentally weak, soft, wishy-washy, a *wimp*;
- indecisive, likely to be pushed around;
- passive;
- physically weak.

FEEDBACK

Feedback is useful in both positive and negative contexts. Examples of positive feedback might include giving recognition for a job well done, or paying someone a sincere compliment. We'll be concentrating on the uses of feedback in dealing with negative or difficult situations.

Use feedback if you've been upset or annoyed by something someone has done. You identify what they're doing that bothers you and give them the opportunity to do something about it. We're being unfair to others when we don't communicate these issues to them.

Consider the following series of events:

- When a person does something that bothers you, a small blip occurs on your "screen of annoyance." Because it's only a small blip you decide to say nothing.
- The person does something else that annoys you, and another, bigger blip occurs on your "screen of annoyance."
- The blips soon accumulate, and you have a major blow-up with the person. The most trivial final incident can trigger this response.

How much better it would have been to handle each blip immediately and keep it from being recorded on your "screen of annoyance."

There are many different times when it is appropriate to use feedback. For example, you should:

- Let others know when you don't understand what they've said.
- Let others know when you like something they've said or done.
- Let others know when you disagree with them.
- Let others know when you think they've changed the subject or are going around in circles.
- Let others know when you're becoming annoyed.
- Let others know when you feel hurt or embarrassed.

Feedback also helps you keep in touch with your reactions, so you can deal with them before they turn into serious negative feelings of frustration, anger, hurt, defensiveness, defeat, fear, depression, dependence, weakness or defenselessness. Most women are comfortable saying that they have such feelings, but men have been socialized to believe it's a weakness to acknowledge them. This limits their options for expressing their feelings. Many respond as if they're angry — an acceptable reaction among men — when in reality, they may feel hurt, or defenseless or afraid. Their ambiguous behaviour confuses women and widens the communication gap between men and women. When men appear upset, often a woman will ask, "What's wrong?" The man's response is often, "Nothing" or "I don't want to talk about it." This makes women feel "shut out" or rejected. This communication gap will be reduced if men stop and analyse what they're really feeling before they react.

Be selective when you use feedback. Ask yourself, "Am I about to unload this gripe properly? Is my reaction unfair or petty?" Feedback must be immediate and specific — don't save up grievances and don't dump too many things on a person at once. As well, there must be something the recipient of the feedback can do about the problem.

To be effective, there must also be a foundation of trust between the sender and receiver of the feedback. Otherwise, the feedback could be misinterpreted as a personal attack. The recipient may hear only critical things and react defensively rather than listen to what you have to say.

Here are some general guidelines for giving feedback:

1. *Be sure the receiver is ready.* Give the feedback only when there are clear indications that the receiver is ready to listen to it. If not, the receiver won't hear it or is likely to misinterpret your comments.
2. *Base your comments on facts, not emotions.* Giving feedback acts like a "candid camera." It's a report of the facts, rather than your ideas about why things happened or what the person meant by them.
3. *Be specific.* Give quotes and examples of exactly what you're referring to.
4. *Give feedback as soon after the event as possible.* The closer you give feedback to the time the event took place, the better. If you give feedback immediately, the receiver is more likely to understand exactly what's meant. The feelings accompanying the event still exist, so this, too, can help.
5. *Pick a convenient time.* Feedback is given when there's a good chance the person will listen to it. It may not be helpful if the receiver feels there are already other matters that demand their attention.
6. *Pick a private place.* Critical feedback given in front of others will be damaging rather than helpful.
7. *Concentrate on what can be changed.* Feedback should be about things that can be changed should the receiver choose to do so.
8. *Request co-operation.* The receiver can consider whether he or she wishes to attempt a change on the basis of your feedback information. You may wish to include that you would like to see certain changes. You're not likely to be successful if you give the impression of saying, "I've told you what's wrong with you, now change!"
9. *Focus on one thing at a time.* When learning how to give feedback, we may sometimes overdo it. It's as though we were telling the receiver, "I just happen to have a list of reactions here. Let me read them off to you." The receiver would naturally prefer time to consider each item and may balk at your overwhelming expectations.

10. *Be helpful.*   Always consider your own motives for giving your opinions. Are you trying to be helpful to the receiver or are you unloading some of your own feelings? Are you using the occasion to try to get the receiver to do something that benefits only you? For example, if you're angry and wish to express it, say so — but include a description of the behaviour that caused your anger.

11. *Encourage the recipient to provide feedback in return.*   Giving feedback can become "one-upmanship." Because the giver has focused on the person's potential for improvement, the receiver goes away feeling as though he or she is "not as good." The exchange will be better balanced if the receiver has a chance to include some of his or her own feelings and concerns.

Here are some guidelines for receiving feedback:

1. *State what you want feedback about.*   Help the giver provide useful reactions by asking for feedback about specific things.
2. *Check what you've heard.*   Use paraphrasing to be sure you understand the giver's message.
3. *Share your reactions to the feedback.*   As your own feelings become involved, you may forget to share your reactions to the feedback you've received. Knowing what was and was not helpful assists the giver to improve his or her ability to provide useful feedback. If the giver is uncertain about your reactions, he or she may be less apt to risk sharing in the future.

Here is an example of how to use feedback:

A receptionist had a problem she didn't know how to handle. She would take messages for all the office staff. One particular client (Mr. Samuels) phoned in repeatedly, asking to speak to Mr. Jacobs. She promptly passed on his messages. The fourth time he called, Mr. Samuels accused her of not passing on his messages to Mr. Jacobs. She wondered how she should deal with this situation as it was likely to happen again. What would you suggest she tell Mr. Samuels the next time he phoned?

Did you notice that she was trying to deal with the wrong problem? Her supervisor, Mr. Jacobs, was the problem, not Mr. Samuels. When I asked her if she had ever considered talking to her supervisor about the problem, she replied, "Oh, I couldn't do that!"

I then asked, "How is the situation going to change unless he knows what his behaviour does to you? You're not even giving him the opportunity of solving this dilemma."

There are three steps in the process of feedback.

1. Describe the problem or situation to the person causing the difficulty.
2. Define what feelings or reactions (anger, sadness, anxiety, hurt or upset) the problem behaviour causes you.
3. Suggest a solution or ask the person to provide a solution.

In the receptionist's case, she might have felt like saying, "You turkey, you never return your telephone messages!" But this kind of accusation would only get her supervisor's back up. Instead, she should try to gain his co-operation in solving the problem. She should say, "I have a problem and I need your help in solving it. Mr. Samuels phoned in four times, and he's really annoyed at me because you haven't returned his calls. This upsets me. What do you suggest I tell him the next time he calls?"

In this transaction, the following feedback steps were taken:

1. The problem — he's not returning his calls.
2. Her feelings or reactions — this upsets me.
3. The solution — she asks Mr. Jacobs to provide one.

Here's another example:

Margo, a co-worker, is always interrupting you with small talk, which interferes with your concentration. You're getting annoyed with her. Your first reaction might be to blast her with a statement such as, "Margo, will you shut up and let me get my work done!" Use feedback instead and say, "Margo, I'm working on an important project. I'm sure you're not aware of this, but every time you interrupt me, I lose my train of thought. Can we talk later at coffee break?"

1. The problem — she's interrupting your work.
2. Your feelings or reactions — you lose your train of thought.
3. The solution — you suggest talking later at coffee break.

Suppose Margo interrupts you again two hours later. What should you tell her? (Remember, this might be a habit with Margo, and she may have done it without thinking.) Your response? Repeat your original comments. "As I mentioned earlier, I'm working on an important project. Every time you interrupt me, I lose my train of thought. Can we talk later at coffee break?"

The next morning, guess what? She's at it again. What should you do now? Many would suggest that you ignore her comments. Instead say, "Margo, twice yesterday I mentioned that I'm working on an important project and your interruptions affected my concentration. Can you tell me why you're still doing this?"

What you're doing is making Margo account for her aggressive actions. (Yes, she's being aggressive, because she now *knows* she's bothering you.) Explain that if it happens again, you'll have to speak to Jim, your supervisor. This is the step most people miss. It explains clearly the consequences Margo will face if she does it again. Margo promises she won't do it again.

Another day goes by, and Margo's at it again! What should you do the fourth time? Don't just say you're going to do something — follow through and talk to your supervisor.

Rather than giving the impression that you're going to "tattle" on your co-worker, ask for your supervisor's advice. Say, "Jim, I have a problem and I need your help in solving it. On Tuesday, I spoke to Margo and asked her to. . . ." Explain everything you've done up to this point to stop her negative behaviour. Then ask, "What do you suggest I do next time she interrupts me?"

Normally, he will talk to Margo himself, because Margo is wasting his department's budget and, ultimately, company money. As Margo reports to Jim, he is ultimately responsible for what she does — and she's making him look bad.

You might ask yourself, "Will Margo like me after I've spoken to my supervisor?" Who cares? She's going to cause you trouble whether you go to your supervisor or not.

Use the wording: "I have a problem and I need your help in

solving it," whenever someone is causing you grief. This is especially effective if used on the person who is causing the problem! You're not shaking your finger at them and bawling them out for their behaviour. You're asking their help in trying to solve it.

This approach often gets the results you're after when other approaches fail. Use this feedback technique whenever a person's pen-clicking, gum-chewing, chair-squeaking or loud voice affects your performance at work. Use it when people are late with their reports, or when their actions keep you from doing your job correctly.

To recap the four major steps in the process of feedback:

1. Follow the three steps from the process of feedback.
2. Repeat step 1.
3. Ask the person to explain why he or she is continuing the annoying behaviour. Explain the consequences should the behaviour or situation happen again.
4. Follow through with the consequences.

Go directly to step 3 if faced with a person who refuses to co-operate.

Using Feedback with Very Difficult People
Among the wide range of human types, there are always a few people who are more difficult to deal with than others. A very difficult person isn't just someone who is having a bad day or with whom you have a personality conflict. A very difficult person is difficult often and with most people.

You *can* use feedback effectively for dealing with such people. However, because the risks are greater that your attempt will backfire, you need to prepare extra carefully before you approach them.

Thorough advance preparation is especially valuable when you're having problems with those in a position of power, such as your supervisor, a parent or an older person.

1. *Determine the problem.* Identify the specific behaviour that's unacceptable; who is affected by the behaviour; and how

frequently it occurs. Concentrate on behaviour the person can do something about. If the problem occurs only with one person, it's most likely a personality conflict rather than difficult behaviour.

2. *Examine relationships.* Clues to the possible causes of the negative behaviour will be found by examining how the difficult person interacts with others. Determining why the behaviour occurs and why it's annoying you will help find solutions.

3. *Determine the cost of the problem behaviour.* Whether it's lost productivity, general discomfort or lower morale, difficult behaviour always carries a cost. The behaviour should be ignored if you can't determine any costs.

4. *Prepare for the confrontation.* Should you have determined that the costs are too high, it's now time to speak to the offender. What special concerns do you have about the problem? What difficulties might you experience in the discussion? How will you handle these problems? Be ready for most situations you may face. Determine what you want to accomplish, then set up a meeting where you'll have privacy and enough time to discuss the situation.

5. *Rehearse thoroughly.* Rehearse the trying situation beforehand with a friend. Your friend should have as much knowledge of the situation as possible. This way, he or she can formulate good arguments and be able to anticipate what the other person's objections or reactions might be. The adage that practice makes perfect works here. Remember that the person you're eventually going to deal with has not had the opportunity to practise.

6. *Find a solution.* In a non-accusatory manner, explain why it concerns you. Give specific facts. Try not to offer your opinion as to why the problem exists. Ask questions to check your understanding. Identify the change in behaviour you're seeking. Be open to changing your solution, if it's inappropriate. Listen to the person's ideas about how he or she can solve the problem. Express confidence in the person's ability to change.

7. *Agree on a plan of action.* Work towards a solution acceptable to both parties.

8. *Obtain a commitment.* Get agreement on specific actions the person will take, and set a deadline for these actions. Ask the

person to confirm that he or she will do what's been agreed upon.

9. *Follow up with the person.* Recognize and comment on any progress you've observed. Re-evaluate the action plan and revise it if necessary. If there's been no change, repeat the process.

Coping strategy

One solution may be to make the best of a bad situation. You can minimize the damage caused by the difficult behaviour by:

- Remaining calm — Don't argue with the other person or make accusations.
- Using your listening skills to check your understanding.
- Being firm — Decide in advance what behaviour you will or will not accept, and don't let yourself be pushed beyond this limit.
- Being persistent and consistent in your response, which conveys to the difficult person that you mean what you say.
- Believing in yourself and your ability to deal with others.
- Looking for ways to lessen your exposure to the behaviour, or to reduce the causes of the behaviour.

LISTENING

We spend up to 80 per cent of our conscious hours using four basic communication skills: writing, reading, speaking and listening. Listening accounts for more than 50 per cent of that time, so we're actually spending 40 per cent of our waking time just listening!

We listen in spurts. Most of us are unable to give close attention to what's being said for more than sixty seconds at a time. We concentrate for a while, our attention lags, then we concentrate again.

Have you ever received specific training on how to listen? Probably not. It was always, "Mary, will you stop talking . . ." not "Mary, will you please listen."

How fast do you think the average person speaks in words per minute? (Keep in mind that secretaries usually take shorthand at 80 to 120 w.p.m. and court stenographers at about 220 w.p.m.)

Normal speaking speed is 125 to 150 w.p.m. My speaking speed is at least 160 w.p.m., even when I'm conducting seminars. This bothered me at one time.

Ask yourself what speed of speech you're capable of listening to? I've heard guesstimates of from 50 to 300 w.p.m. In reality, we're capable of listening at the phenomenal speed of 750 to 1,200 w.p.m.!

Then why don't we hear what people tell us? Because we're bored — that's why. There's not enough to keep our brain occupied when people speak at normal speeds. Even my speaking speed of 160 w.p.m. can't keep participants motivated during a seminar all the time. So what happens? We all go on side-trips where we may:

- start finding examples of something the person's discussing;
- wonder why our spouse was in such a bad mood that morning;
- admire something someone is wearing and wonder where they bought it;
- wonder if it's time for coffee break.

Radio and television have turned most of us into lazy listeners. For instance, did you turn the radio on this morning to catch the weather forecast or the news? Did you hear it? Or did you tune out the voices and miss it entirely? It takes practice and concentration to stay "tuned in" to what's being said.

There are several "problem listeners" that we all have to deal with. Here are a few.

Kinds of Bad Listeners
- *Bashful people.* Because shy people expect others to draw them out, they place emotional demands on everyone they're with. If they don't receive this attention, they tune out. Most shy people aren't aware of this negative behaviour, nor of the demands it places on others around them.
- *Anxious people.* Because they lack confidence, they are nervous chatterers. They worry about what *they're* going to say next, which leaves little room for listening to others.
- *Argumentative people.* They'd argue with Einstein about his

theory of relativity! They nitpick small details, which breaks conversational flow.

- *Opinionated people*. They spend their energy formulating arguments, rather than listening to others. They interrupt and begin every other sentence with "but . . . ." These people may be overly anxious to impress others, but they often produce the opposite effect. People "tune them out."
- *Closed-minded people*. The most infuriating of bad listeners: they have rigid sets of values and find security in their prejudices. Any new ideas or changes leave them feeling threatened.

When faced with these poor listeners, use feedback to explain how you feel. Use of tact and empathy will assist you in helping them to become better listeners. Explain to closed-minded people that they've literally shut you out, that their unwillingness to listen to your ideas makes you feel rejected and unimportant. If you explain this, and the person continues to behave the same way, you can (a) put up with it, or (b) use steps 2 to 4 of *Feedback Steps*.

Most poor listeners aren't aware of their failing. Your feedback may be helpful in changing their attitude and behaviour.

Blocks to Effective Listening

There are other things that can lead you astray when listening. Ask yourself which ones are problems for you:

- You had trouble understanding the speaker's words or lacked the knowledge to grasp the message. (The speaker was using unfamiliar language, jargon or technical terms.)
- You were thinking of what you were going to say while the speaker was talking.
- You were preoccupied with how strongly you disagreed with the speaker's views.
- You listened for what you wanted to hear.
- You were too tired mentally to work at paying attention.
- There were outside noises and distractions.
- The speaker had poor delivery — slow, windy, irrelevant, rambling or repetitious.

- Something the speaker said intrigued you; you thought about it, and when you tuned back in, you'd lost the thread.
- The speaker had an accent that you found difficult to understand.
- You tuned out because you thought you knew what the speaker's conclusions were going to be.
- You forgot to use paraphrasing and feedback in listening effectively.
- You felt you were being given far too much information.

How Do You Rate as a Listener?

Rate yourself (or have a friend help you) using the following scale:
Always = 5   Almost always = 4   Sometimes = 3
Rarely = 2   Never = 1

1. I allow the speaker to express his or her complete thoughts without interrupting. _____
2. I actively try to develop my ability to remember important facts. _____
3. In a conference or important phone conversation, I write down the most important details of a message. _____
4. I avoid becoming hostile or excited if a speaker's views differ from mine. _____
5. I repeat the essential details of a conversation back to the speaker to confirm that I have understood correctly. _____
6. I exercise tact in keeping the speaker on track. _____
7. I tune out distractions when listening. _____
8. I make an effort to show interest in the other person's conversation. _____
9. I understand that I'm learning little when I'm talking. (I talk too much, listen too little?) _____
10. I sound as if I'm listening. (I use paraphrasing, ask questions.) _____
11. I remember that people are less defensive when they feel they're being understood. _____
12. I understand that I don't have to agree with the speaker. _____
13. In personal conversation, I look for non-verbal forms of communication, such as body language, tone of voice and other signals that provide information in addition to the speaker's words. _____

14. I look as if I'm listening in personal meetings. (I lean forward, give eye contact.) _____
15. I ask for the spelling of names and places when I'm taking a message. _____

Scoring: 64 or more — You're an excellent listener!
       50-63   — You're better than average.
       40-49   — You require improvement!
       39 or less — You're not an effective listener.
                      You need practice, practice
                      and more practice!

To elaborate on question 12: Suppose, in a conversation with someone about a controversial topic (such as abortion or capital punishment) you discover the two of you are on opposite sides of the issue. If your discussion is going nowhere but is making both of you angry, say: "You're entitled to your opinion, and I'm entitled to my opinion. Let's agree to disagree, and not discuss it any more."

To elaborate on question 15: When you're taking down people's names, ask them to confirm the spelling (even the name Smith may be spelled Smythe). In brackets (below the spelling of the name) add your own phonetic pronunciation of the name. For instance, the last name TOZER would be phonetically *Toe-zer*; BLECHA — *Blek-ka*; CARPHIN — *Car-fin*; CEBULIAK — *Ceb-u-luck*.

This technique is very helpful to the person who will be returning the call. I use it on client files, so that I pronounce the person's name properly when I contact him or her in the future.

How to Improve Your Listening Skills

1. You must care enough to want to improve. Without this motivation, it'll be too much effort.
2. Try to find an uninterrupted area in which to converse. Keeping your train of thought is difficult when there are obstructions to concentration.
3. Try not to anticipate what the other person will say.
4. Be mindful of your own biases and prejudices, so they don't unduly influence your listening.
5. Pay careful attention to what's being said. Don't stop listening in order to plan a rebuttal to a particular point.

6. Be aware of "red flag" words that might trigger an overreaction or a stereotyped reaction. Examples of this are "women's libber" or "male chauvinist."
7. Don't allow yourself to get too far ahead of the speaker by trying to understand things too soon.
8. At intervals, try to paraphrase what people have been saying. Give them the opportunity to learn what you think you've heard them say.
9. When you have difficulty determining the point of the speaker's remarks, say, "Why are you telling me this?"
10. Watch for key or buzz words if you find you've lost the train of the conversation. This happens particularly when the speaker is long-winded or has a tendency to ramble.
11. Don't interrupt to demand clarification of insignificant or irrelevant details.

Qualities of a Good Listener
People who practise good listening skills do the following:
1. Let others finish what they're saying without interrupting them.
2. Ask questions if they're confused.
3. Pay attention to what others are saying and show they're paying attention by keeping comfortable eye contact. They don't let their eyes wander around the room.
4. Remain open-minded, ready to revise their opinion.
5. Use feedback and paraphrasing skills.
6. Pay attention to non-verbal signals such as the speaker's body language.
7. Don't "tune out" inappropriately when others are speaking.

SPEAKING
Another communication skill is the art of being able to say what you want to say. Verbal fluency enables you to express your thoughts clearly so others understand exactly what you mean. Here is a test you can give yourself. As we often don't see ourselves clearly, it might be a benefit to have a friend do it for you as well.

How Do You Rate as a Speaker?

Rate yourself using the following scale:
Always = 5   Almost always = 4   Sometimes = 3
Rarely = 2   Never = 1

1. If I were a listener, I would listen to myself. _____
2. If I'm being misunderstood, I remember that it's my responsibility to help the other person understand me. _____
3. I keep my instructions to others short, sweet and to the point. _____
4. I am aware of when my audience has tuned me out. _____
5. I make sure my listeners know what I want from them. _____
6. When I give instructions, I ask for feedback and para-phrasing to make sure I'm understood. _____
7. I make sure my non-verbal signals (body language, tone of voice, etc.) are the same as my verbal ones. _____
8. I make sure I don't intimidate my listeners with a loud voice, threatening appearance, intense or prolonged eye contact, verbal attacks, etc. _____
9. I articulate clearly. _____
10. I try to use language the listener can understand. _____

Scoring: 40 or more — You're an excellent speaker!
         32-39 — You're better than average.
         25-31 — You require improvement!
         24 or less — You're not an effective speaker. You need practice, practice, and more practice!

Did you chuckle to yourself when responding to the first statement? Did you find there was an element of truth in it? It's possible that you are one of those people who believe they're not worth listening to. There are three main reasons why you may feel you're not a good speaker.

1. *You have trouble getting the words out.* Some people know what they want to say, but can't quite say it. (They lack verbal fluency.) You could try joining Toastmaster or Toastmistress clubs or take a public-speaking course. Because you're going to be talking the rest of your life, it certainly seems worthwhile to improve this essential communication skill.

2. *You're not up on what's going on.*   Often people insulate themselves from anything outside their own little world. Then, in social situations, they find they're not up on current events and have nothing to contribute to the conversation. The solution is to catch up on what's happening.
3. *You're a "motor-mouth."*   Some people have problems keeping conversations short, sweet and to the point. Take the time to organize your thoughts before you speak. Practise by writing down your thoughts, or use a tape recorder. Then reword your remarks, using more precise language.

The suggestions in point (3) will also be useful if you have trouble giving clear instructions. Use the KISS principle: Keep It Simple, Sweetie (or Keep It Simple, Stupid — depending on how you feel at the time).

To ensure that your listeners know what you want from them, ask them for their help before you give them the background information. For example:

A man wanted to discuss a work problem with his wife, who had just put in a rather tiring day herself. He proceeded to give her all kinds of details about what was happening. When he asked, "What do you think I should do?", she was embarrassed, because she had been only half-listening. He had to tell her all the details again before she could answer. How much better it would have been, if he had started out the conversation, "Mary, I need your opinion on something that's happening at the office. Do you have time to discuss it right now?" Then he would have confirmed that she did have time, and she would have been aware that he needed her undivided attention.

CHAPTER THREE

COMMUNICATION TECHNIQUES FOR SPECIFIC SITUATIONS

ACCENTUATING THE POSITIVE

A "warm glow" is one of the nicest things we can give to others, be they customers, friends, family or co-workers. These are positive comments that give nice feelings to the recipient (and usually the giver as well).

We give warm glows when we pay authentic compliments to others. Nothing makes others feel better about themselves than to receive praise for a job well done. This has a dual benefit, because people enjoy being around complimentary people. If you give recognition when recognition is due, others feel comfortable when you're around.

We can give warm glows to others by simply using proper manners. Unfortunately, we seldom remember this when dealing with family members or those close to us (a time when we should!). After all, who's more important to us than our family, relatives, close friends and co-workers? You can give co-workers a warm glow by thanking them for doing something extra for you. When friends and family go out of their way to do something for you, remember to thank them too.

Even if the favour was done two weeks ago and you still haven't said anything, it's not too late. In fact, an unexpected late comment such as, "Bill, I forgot to thank you for the information you sent me. I used it in my proposal for a new client, and they loved it!" can do wonders for the recipient's morale.

You can give clients warm glows by remembering their names and paying attention to what they're saying.

Should you keep a warm glow? No. Pass it on to someone else. Most people have more trouble remembering their last warm glow than the opposite – their last "dampener".

ELIMINATING THE NEGATIVE

Unlike warm glows, "dampeners" make people feel bad about a situation or themselves. Sometimes we provoke hostile reactions from others by the way we treat them. They *become* difficult people in response to something we've done. For example, you give a dampener to others when you:

- keep them waiting unnecessarily either on the phone or in person;
- move more slowly than necessary when serving others;
- forget regular clients' names;
- forget to say please and thank you.

Such actions and oversights convey the impression that the recipient is unimportant, almost a non-person. Such behaviour is degrading to both of you. Everyone has the same rights as you do and deserves to be treated with the same respect you yourself expect to receive from others.

Should you keep a dampener? No. Mentally throw it in the garbage can. But don't pass it on, even when everyone else seems to. When people take out their bad feelings on you, remember that you can choose not to accept the dampener. Passing the bad feeling on to someone else just makes for two unhappy people instead of one.

NEUTRALIZING MEAN MANIPULATORS

People use "put-downers" when they give a compliment, then discount it by saying something negative. Some use disguised or obvious put-downs that are meant to hurt. When dealing with these people, use the following formula:

1. After receiving the put-down, reflect your understanding of the situation. Say, "You feel/think/believe. . . ." This confirms that you heard what they said to you (a form of paraphrasing).
2. Then state, "I understand/perceive/appreciate/empathize with/realize that. . . ." Then express *their* point of view as you perceive it.
3. Make an assertive statement, such as "I think/feel/believe/have . . . ," and state *your* beliefs about the topic. Don't start your statement with such words as "but," "however," "although" or "nevertheless."
4. Ask an open question (one that can't be answered by a yes or a no).

Here is an example of how to deal with a discriminatory statement regarding age:

Commenter: "You're pretty young to be a supervisor, aren't you?"

You: "You feel that I'm too young to be a supervisor?"

Commenter: "Well, you are young!"

You: "I understand what you mean. I have six years' experience in this department. I also have a BA degree and have completed all the supervisory training provided by our company. What other qualifications do you feel I need to handle my position?"

Tone of voice is very important in these exchanges. Your voice should indicate not defensiveness, but simply that you're stating facts. This starts a dialogue where facts are discussed rather than emotions displayed.

Suppose you are the recipient of a racial slur:

Commenter: "Every time I take a cab, the driver is always Asian. Can't you people find anything else to do other than drive taxis?"

You: "You feel that people from Asia should have jobs other than driving a taxi. I realize why you must believe that. Many people from my country have to obtain extra education to work at their usual occupations in Great Britain. I'm taking university courses and will soon be working in my normal kind of job. What kind of special courses did you take to work in your kind of job?"

Here is a gender-related example.

Commenter: "You're earning a good salary for a woman."
You: "You believe that women should earn less than men?"
Commenter: "Yes, I do."
You: "I understand what you're saying. I believe women deserve an equal chance to earn the same kind of salary as men. Women pay rent like men, pay the same for food as men, and certainly pay taxes like men. What are the reasons for your belief that women should earn less than men?"

Use this technique for any disguised or obvious put-downs.

BEING CONSTRUCTIVE
Of course it is sometimes necessary to discuss people's mistakes — in other words, to criticize them. Criticism can be either *destructive* — just making the person feel worthless — or *constructive* — offering specific suggestions for improvement.

Think about the last rip-snorting argument you had with someone. Did you label the *person*, or did you play fair and discuss the person's *behaviour*?

For example, you could say: "John, how could you do such a dumb thing?" That's labelling John without giving him any information about how to stop being "dumb."

Or you could say: "John, you didn't spend much time preparing your report, did you? It turned out to be useless, and I had to do it over again." That's discussing his behaviour and giving him specific information about how he can change it.

In an argument, if you find yourself labelling someone, please apologize to them. Say, "I'm sorry. You didn't deserve that. What I meant was. . . ." You can then discuss the behaviour that offended you using the feedback technique.

If people label you, ask for specific reasons why they have given you the label. Remember you have the choice of accepting or not accepting the criticism.

We can decide not to allow people to hurt us. A co-worker may betray us, gossip about us, or try to give us guilt trips. It's not easy to forgive this behaviour. We may feel that we're letting ourselves down if we forgive others too easily. We may feel we should wait for them to do something to mend the rift. We may be tempted to dwell to an unhealthy extent on the injury we feel they have done us.

In many cases, however, forgiving is the only thing that will mend and heal. Forgiving can actually lead to a renewed relationship.

You may say, "That's easy for you to say! Your co-worker didn't gossip behind your back and pass on untrue information about you!"

Here's what you can do to mend the rift. Stop pretending that you like the person. Acknowledge to yourself that you are angry, and examine why. Then be direct with the other person, telling him or her frankly what has offended you. Keep in mind, however, that the person is only human, and that we all make mistakes. Then make a conscious decision to forgive and forget. (You have to mean it.) Once you forgive the person, you can get on with your life.

Many people don't agree with this approach. They believe that forgiving wrongdoers just lets them off the hook — it's too easy on them. In reality, however, holding a grudge ties the injured party to the wrongdoer. Anger and hate use up energy that should be spent positively in picking up the pieces.

I found that I could get on with my life when I forgave others for injuries done to me. Ironically, in my case, all these people have subsequently had problems resulting directly from their own hurtful behaviour. For instance, one boss I had was afraid that I might be after his job. He made my life a living hell for months, which caused terrible stress and health problems for me. I finally had to admit defeat and look for work elsewhere. That man is now bouncing from one job to another, each at a lower level than the one before. He leaves behind a string of former co-workers who despise him.

Accepting Compliments
Many of us have difficulty receiving compliments graciously. We

discount or refuse to accept them with such comments as: "Oh, I could have done better" or "This old rag?"

If you don't accept compliments graciously, what are you telling the person giving you the compliment? You're implying that he or she is insincere or has poor judgment. You repaid a warm glow (a good feeling) with a dampener (a bad feeling). Remember this the next time you discount a compliment.

Counselling Others

Listening skills come in handy if you're asked for advice. You can feel free to give expert or professional advice when you're an expert in a field; however, when others come to you with personal problems, don't make the mistake of giving advice! This approach is also excellent for people who are whiners and complainers. It gets them on the road to solving their problem. Should they bother you with the same problem or situation in the future, remind them of the steps you went through with them. You might even say, "You know what you have to do to solve this problem. I don't want to hear another word about it until you do what you know you have to do to solve it." Here are the recommended steps to take when asked for advice or called upon to counsel others for personal problems:

1. Have them explain the problem to you in detail.
2. Ask them what solutions they think will solve the problem. (You can suggest other ideas that they may not have thought of.)
3. Ask them to identify the advantages and disadvantages of each solution.
4. Ask them which solution makes the most sense to them, but don't suggest what you would do, even if asked to do so.
5. Write specific steps they will take to solve the problem (goal setting).

Why isn't it a good idea to suggest what you would do? The person might follow your advice and, if the results are bad, you will feel you are at least partly responsible.

By using the recommended steps, you help the person be more independent. He or she will become better at working through problems by themselves. Supervisors should use this when asked for advice. Before automatically stepping in and giving the answer, they should ask, "What do you think you should do?" This gives the person the opportunity to test his or her ideas, which results in more independent decision making. That person will come to you less often for advice.

A cartoon I once saw showed a very upset man entering a door labelled "counsellor." He was shown talking with the counsellor, then leaving the room with a smile on his face. The next picture showed a back view of the counsellor. She had a wind-up key in her back, which made her head nod. To me this suggests that often just having someone to listen while you talk about a problem can help in solving the problem. Learn to be one of those good listeners, and you'll have many friends.

Avoiding Ambiguous Messages

Sometimes our words and behaviour are open to more than one interpretation. If we don't realize this and clarify our intended meaning, our behaviour can be misinterpreted. Here's an example:

1. *Supervisor's Intention.* A supervisor wants to let Mary (one of his staff) know that he recognizes and appreciates the extra load she's been carrying lately. He debates which of the following would best communicate his appreciation:
   a. giving Mary some time off;
   b. taking Mary out to lunch;
   c. telling Mary how he feels;
   d. trying to reduce Mary's workload.
2. *Supervisor's Action.* He decides on d, and eases up on Mary's work load.
3. *Mary's Reaction.* Mary notices the reduced work load, but doesn't know what it means. Her supervisor might be:
   a. criticizing her for not having kept up with her work load;
   b. trying to tell her she shouldn't spend so much time on the phone;
   c. trying to be helpful;
   d. convinced she can't handle crisis situations.

4. *Effect on Mary.* She decides it's a, and feels hurt and put down.
5. *Mary Encodes:* I'm not going to let him know that he's hurt me. Shall I:
   a. say nothing?
   b. say thanks?
6. *Mary's Action.* She decides to say thanks.
7. *Effect on Supervisor.* He believes that Mary understands and appreciates what he's done.

This is a classic example of how ambiguous behaviour can be misunderstood. The supervisor's intention was positive and caring. However, the effect on his employee was the direct opposite of what he wanted. How much better it would have been if he had backed his actions up with words. By using positive feedback, he would have made sure Mary knew why he was easing her workload.

The following example illustrates the sometimes serious consequences that can result from failure to explain ambiguous behaviour. A company was doing well, even though the economy was down. The company had decided to move its facilities to a larger, more comfortable building. The good news was to be announced to employees at a special meeting planned for 5:00 p.m. Thursday. The problems began when workers from another company came to the reception desk Monday morning. They told the receptionist that they were there to measure the offices. When asked why, they explained, "Because the new owners need this information before they move in."

After checking with her office manager, the receptionist gave permission to the workers to measure the offices. She began having the awful feeling that she might be out of a job soon. At coffee break, she mentioned the situation to two other co-workers, who of course passed this information on to others. By Tuesday afternoon, word reached the company executives that half their staff were applying for jobs with other companies and thought Thursday's meeting would announce the folding of their company. Management quickly decided to announce the good news on Tuesday at 5:00 p.m.

Dealing with Language Barriers

Until they become completely fluent in English, people who speak English as a second language normally go through the following process:

Stage 1. They hear what you say in English.
Stage 2. They translate what you've said into their first language.
Stage 3. They construct their answer in their first language.
Stage 4. They mentally translate the answer into English.
Stage 5. They reply to you in English.

You can see that this process takes time, so if you're conversing with someone whose second language is English, try to:

1. Use simple, ordinary language. You can't expect them to learn jargon or technical language right away.
2. Watch their body language. If they frown, you may have lost them. Repeat what you said, using simpler language.
3. Allow them time to interpret what you've said. The "pregnant pause" between the end of your speech and the beginning of their response may be necessary for complete understanding on their part.

Sometimes, no matter what you do, you may find it impossible to understand what someone is saying to you. Whenever possible, try to find someone who speaks the person's language. If that's not possible, ask the person to bring along someone (perhaps a child or a relative) who can act as an interpreter.

If this is a recurring problem, check government offices to see if they have interpreters available to translate. Refer the caller to this service.

Catch yourself if you have guilt feelings. If you've done everything you can to understand the person, you have no reason to accept any guilt feelings.

In the past I had the misfortune of having to deal with a receptionist who had a very strong foreign accent. I couldn't understand what she was saying, and don't think she could understand me. This problem continued for about two weeks. I wasn't able to conduct business properly with the company. I finally decided to do something, and asked to speak to the office manager. I explained my dilemma as follows:

"I have a problem and I need your help in solving it. Several times in the past two weeks I've called your company and have had difficulty understanding what your new receptionist was saying. Have others complained to you about this? You may be losing clients because of it."

She admitted she had heard rumblings from co-workers in the office, but said I was the first complaint from outside the company. She assured me that she would solve the problem. The next time I called the company, a new person answered the phone. If I hadn't complained, the situation might have gone on much longer, with clients lost for this company along the way.

Dealing with Persistent People

In this age of tele-marketing, we've all encountered telephone salespeople. For example, you're probably familiar with the sweet young thing who wants to explain her company's rug-cleaning special. When she identifies herself and asks how your day is going, you know that a sales pitch will follow. I suggest using the following technique:

The stuck record

"We have a special on rug cleaning today."

"Thank you for calling, but I'm not interested."

"But this special is just good for this week . . ."

"I'm not interested."

"How about having your living-room suite cleaned?"

"I'm not interested. . . . Goodbye." You hang up.

Many might feel that this person is just trying to make a living. My answer to this is that they're invading my privacy. If I want rug cleaning, I'll call and ask for it.

With the stuck-record technique, you simply repeat the same thing over and over again. You don't raise your voice, or get defensive. By the third refusal, the salesperson usually accepts that you're serious.

This technique also works well in an office if you're the one who has to fend off salespeople. Let's say your instructions are to accept only a person's business card and catalogue (or information on their product). Someone from your company will follow up if the offered product or service is of interest.

Here's how to handle the next salesperson:

"I'd like to see the office manager please."

"Do you have an appointment?"

"No, I don't."

"Could you please tell me the reason for your visit?"

"I'd like to explain our product to your office manager."

"My instructions are to accept any information you'd care to leave. The office manager will call you if she's interested."

"Our special is only on this week."

"Leave the information with me, and the office manager will call you if she's interested."

"I'm sure she would want to see me."

"Leave the information with me, and the office manager will call you if she's interested [you hold out a hand for the information]. Thank you."

You can use this technique in other situations too — for instance, when someone is trying to convince you to do something you really don't want to do.

"Harry, can you drive me home from work tonight?"

"No I can't, sorry. I'm busy."

"Harry, I really need you to drive me home from work tonight. How come you can't drive me?"

"As I said, I'm too busy."

When anyone asks you to explain why you've said no, they're acting aggressively and are trying to take advantage of you. You're under no obligation to tell people why you can't do what they want you to do. Use this technique whenever you want to say no to somebody who's trying to convince you to say yes. No guilt feelings!

No Isn't a Dirty Word

Do you say yes for any of the following reasons?

- You don't want to hurt someone's feelings.
- You don't want to explain why you want to say no.

- You don't want to say anything the other person might interpret as negative.
- You feel compelled to spend time with the person because you haven't seen her or him in months.
- The other person is particularly important to you.
- You would really like to oblige, but the timing is inappropriate.

Learning how to say no when you want to depends on increasing:

— your self-respect;
— your confidence about following your own standards and decisions;
— your comfort about meeting your own personal needs;
— your understanding that your worth does not depend on other people's judgments;
— your comfort and confidence in pleasing yourself;
— your understanding that you can't always please everyone.

Try the following, should you have trouble saying no when you need to. Each step forward can help you learn when and how to say no comfortably.

How to Say No

Step 1. Pick one type of situation where you've said yes inappropriately several times during the past few months. Concentrate on this area first.

Step 2. Identify your reasons for saying yes. Are you concerned that saying no might injure the relationship? Are you worried about the other person's feelings?

Step 3. Put together a plan of action for preventing this next time. Part of this step involves preparing yourself for such an occasion. Part involves preventing the occasion from recurring.

Step 4. Practise your new response. Get in touch with how you sound and feel as you say no in a skilful and thoughtful way. Rehearse with an uninvolved person who has good judgment.

NOTE: Always know what you want before you decide to say yes.

Don't allow yourself to feel compelled to return a favour from a friend. Stop saying yes to people just because you believe saying no will hurt their feelings.

Understanding Non-Verbal Signals

You notice that the friend you're having lunch with has some food on the corner of her mouth. You want to bring this to her attention in a tactful way. You take your napkin and wipe your own face, but at the same time look at your friend's face where the food is. In many cases she will wipe her face too, though she wouldn't be able to explain why she did so.

We "hear" what people say partly through what their body language, tone of voice, etc., tell us. Being able to interpret non-verbal signals is probably one of the best assets anyone can have. If you want to be a good communicator, it's essential to be aware of and try to understand such non-verbal signals. The only people who can lie consistently without having their body language give them away are con artists and compulsive liars. This is because they actually believe the lies they're telling. Here are some examples of what body language can tell us:

- *Tapping fingers.* The person is annoyed, impatient or anxious.
- *Shifting weight from one foot to another.* The person has been standing too long, or is impatient.
- *Frowning.* The person doesn't understand what's being said or disagrees with what's being said.
- *Flushed face.* The person is embarrassed, angry or hot, or has high blood pressure. You'd have to look for other non-verbal signs to confirm which one it was.
- *Clenched jaw.* The person is upset, angry or anxious. This signal is more common in men than women.
- *Hand cupped around ear.* The person didn't hear what you said.
- *Slumped posture.* The person is tired, relaxed or depressed.
- *Avoidance of eye contact.* The person is shy, or bored. Or the person is from a culture that regards eye contact with the elderly or those in positions of authority as disrespectful. This signal is

often misinterpreted as a sign of shifty behaviour or a lack of self-confidence, when the cause may be something quite different.

- *Rapid or abrupt speech.* The person is upset, worried, anxious or angry.
- *Rise in voice volume.* The person is nervous or angry.
- *Rise in voice pitch.* A sign in women that the person is nervous or angry.
- *Drop in voice pitch.* A sign in men that the person is nervous or angry.
- *Jumpy body movements.* The person is nervous, anxious or angry.
- *Nose scratching.* The person is puzzled or dislikes something. Or the person's nose may be itchy.
- *Shrugging.* The person is indifferent or doesn't know the answer.
- *Forehead slapping.* The person feels forgetful or stupid.
- *Arms across chest.* The person feels defensive, physically cold or physically awkward. This may frequently be seen when men sit in chairs without arms.
- *Back slapping.* The person is offering congratulations, or perhaps encouragement.
- *Thumb and forefinger circling.* The person is saying "Okay," or "Right!" In some cultures this is seen as an obscene gesture.
- *Holding the hand up, palm outwards.* This means "Stop!"
- *Clasping both hands over head.* The person feels triumphant, pleased, successful.
- *Poking you in the ribs.* The person is sharing a joke or teasing you.

We often place our hand on the arm or shoulder of an upset person. With close friends, relatives, children or elderly persons, we might put an arm around their shoulder or hug them to give comfort.

We shake hands with people, an important non-verbal exchange. Originally, this communication meant that we were extending our empty weapon hand to show that we came as a friend. Now it can mean that we are giving our word that the exchange to follow is above board; that we are trustworthy. Women in business should practise until they feel comfortable giving a firm handshake. At a job interview, candidates should offer their hand first, rather than wait for the interviewer to do so. This indicates a high degree of self-confidence in a way that's hard to duplicate.

When you're interested in what others are saying, you might lean forward. You might also lean forward when you wish to speak next.

When people feel they are in a position of power, they often show dominance by deliberately interrupting others. They stand with feet straddled, hands on hips (a parental stance). They may fail to step aside when on a collision course with others. They may hold eye contact longer than is comfortable for the recipient, or hover or lean over others while watching them work. (If someone does this to you, stop working and use the feedback technique to explain what their behaviour is doing to you.)

Men who want to show their power will straddle a chair. Others will put their feet up on a desk and ostentatiously not remove them when someone comes into the room.

Power-hungry people take up more space on couches or benches than is their due. Don't encourage people to do this at the expense of others. Do something!

I remember one time when I had been travelling all day and was bone tired. There was a one-hour wait between connections at an airport. The place was crowded with travellers. I spotted a man sitting at one end of a bench. Taking up the rest of the bench were his briefcase, suitcase and overcoat.

I approached him and asked, "Is this your briefcase?" He nodded. I removed the briefcase from the bench and placed it in front of him.

"Is this your suitcase?" He nodded. I removed the suitcase from the bench and placed it in front of him.

Before I could ask him, "Is this your overcoat?" he removed it and placed it on his lap. I smiled and sat down right next to him.

Shortly after, two other tired travellers joined us on the bench. Their body language and smiles thanked me for the effort I had made.

People who lack assurance show this by their body language as well. Their posture shows defeat, there's little eye contact, their voices are soft. They take up as little space as possible (pull all their "ends" in) or wear a fixed smile.

People who are lying may give themselves away through non-verbal signals. When people are being open with you, their body language usually indicates openness. They show their hands openly, for example. When they are hiding something, their body language changes. They may hide their hands in their pockets or behind their backs. If you accuse them of something, they'll likely give you an incredulous look and reply, "Who me?" They may put their hand on their chest (a non-verbal sign of honesty. NOTE: The hand-to-the-chest gesture when used by women may also be a protective gesture showing sudden surprise or shock), but other body language may contradict this. Look for signals such as:

— avoiding eye contact (usually by looking down)
— blinking rapidly
— twitching and swallowing repeatedly
— clearing the throat and wetting the lips often
— covering the mouth when speaking
— shrugging
— rubbing the nose
— scratching the head while talking
— putting a hand on the throat
— rubbing the back of the neck

To Touch or Not to Touch

The book *The Silent Language*, by Dr. Edward T. Hall, shows that conditioning and cultural backgrounds strongly affect our body language and our responses to others' body language. For instance, it's known that Italian people touch much more often than the British, who back away from this perceived familiarity. They may think of Italian people as pushy; in turn, Italians may think of them as cold or reserved. If you deal with people of other cultures, *The Silent Lanuage* is a book well worth reading.

In this day when the issue of sexual harassment is receiving growing attention, many people avoid initiating any physical contact at all with their co-workers. Nevertheless, touch can be a valuable and often therapeutic form of communication. Especially for those working in the health-care industries, it is important to know when it is appropriate to make use of this form of non-verbal communication.

The bereaved
Adults are likely to put up barricades to hide hurt feelings. They may need verbal reassurance before they'll let others comfort them physically. This could happen to a person when a family member or close friend dies. Bereaved people really need comforting, but may push others away. This can be because they feel too vulnerable to trust others with their feelings. They're afraid they'll fall apart if they feel any more emotion, so they may literally push others away, or remain rigid when people try to comfort them. Please don't give up — watch for non-verbal signs that they're ready for physical comforting.

The elderly
Elderly people in nursing homes may often be observed stroking the bedcovers or some other soft fabric.

For many senior citizens the luxury of being touched by others is missing. Sure, they receive attention from the staff, but it may be rare for anyone to touch them lovingly. Relatives and friends come to visit, but may not even offer to hold their hand.

Affectionate touching from others is a life-long need. If others are cranky or miserable, one of the reasons could be that this necessity of life is missing from their lives.

Patients in hospital
When people are hospitalized, they may have feelings of being isolated and notice the lack of comforting physical touching. They also may feel apprehensive, frightened and fearful of what will happen or has happened to them in this unfamiliar territory.

A caring pat on the shoulder or someone to hold their hand may be important to their speedy recovery. Nothing combats the loneliness of being in the hospital so well as loved ones who provide comfort and reassurance. Fill that need whenever you visit anyone in the hospital. Even a casual friend welcomes a pat on the arm or some other physical gesture that shows you care. If you work in the health-care business, the evening back-rub provides the ideal opportunity to give the touching.

Space bubbles

We all have a "space bubble" around us — a gap between us and others that we need to maintain to feel secure. For most people, this bubble extends eighteen to twenty-four inches from their bodies.

There are several types of distances we normally keep between ourselves and others. These are:

- *Intimate distance.* Only people we trust are welcome within our "space bubble." We welcome people who are near and dear to us into this space, but we often have to endure others as well. This can be at the theatre, on a bus, at a seminar or in an elevator. You can probably think of hundreds of instances where we have to tolerate this closeness.

    Watch yourself when you're in an elevator. You naturally pull in all your *ends* and take up as little space as possible. Should you inadvertently touch the stranger next to you, you'll automatically say, "Oops, I'm sorry," and pull away. This would also happen if you touched someone in a bank lineup, or at a checkout counter.
- *Personal distance* is the space you usually keep with others when you have enough room to be comfortable. This is anywhere between three and four feet, depending on your comfort zone and how well you know the person. In elevators, as soon as the crowd thins, people will automatically widen the space between themselves and others.
- *Social distance* is four to seven feet. Strangers or acquaintances sitting on chairs or couches at a party will try to maintain this distance.
- *Far social distance.* This could happen at a large party or be the distance between a speaker and his or her audience.
- *Territorial supremacy.* Not only do we try to keep a certain quantity of space around us, but also we try to retain physical control over anything we think belongs to us. This may be a desk at work; our bedroom, kitchen or workshop; our car or boat; or our brush and comb. Others may use these articles only

when we've given them permission to do so. That is why we may react violently when someone takes something of ours without permission.

The office receptionist is often the victim of "territorial invasions." Other office workers somehow think that it's okay to help themselves to the bottle of correcting fluid or the stapler on her desk. They may even open her desk drawers and help themselves to her scissors or ruler. Try to remember that that desk is *hers*. Don't take anything that you haven't asked permission to use. Should *you* be the receptionist, designate a communal area where such equipment can be kept. For example, keep an extra bottle of correcting fluid, a ruler, a stapler and a pair of scissors on top of a filing cabinet. Make others aware that equipment in this area is theirs, while your desk is *yours*.

People have the psychological upper hand when they're in their own territory. Salespeople are very aware of this. If the client comes to the seller's place of business, the seller has the advantage. If the salesperson goes to the potential client's place of business, the client has the advantage. That is why salespeople often try to find a neutral ground on which to sell their products.

This psychological truth also holds when a supervisor has to discipline an employee. If the situation isn't serious, the supervisor will likely go to the employee's territory, so that the employee will feel less threatened, or will arrange to discuss the matter on neutral territory, such as an empty office or a cafeteria. Privacy is a must in all cases.

With a more serious problem, the supervisor will most likely have the employee come to his or her office, where he or she will have more power and the employee will feel less secure. There are degrees of intimidation here, too. For the employee, the least threatening environment in the supervisor's office is at a round table of some sort. Next is beside the supervisor's desk. In the most threatening arrangement the supervisor is behind the desk with the subordinate sitting opposite. To increase the quelling effect the supervisor might arrange for the subordinate to sit in a lower chair than the supervisor. Or a supervisor who is small in stature might stand up to give a more powerful impression.

Eye contact

Variations in eye contact convey a great deal. Comfortable eye contact is three seconds. If you hold eye contact longer than three seconds, you are invading another's body space as directly as if you had touched him or her. Many aggressive people use a fixed stare to intimidate others. They could be one hundred feet away from you, but you'd still feel their invasion of your space.

You may have used extended eye contact yourself when you've been very angry with someone. You looked them right in the eye as you spoke to them. If a person says, "He was shooting darts at me," that person was probably giving full eye contact for too long, possibly reinforced by an angry expression.

Blinking eyes may indicate either lying or nervousness. Unblinking eyes with eye contact could mean the person is lying and watching for your reaction. Or the person could be intensely interested in what you're saying.

A wink can show either intimacy or lack of seriousness. The latter may be directed at parents when you're telling a "white lie" to their child.

Arguments

Should you have to referee an argument, I suggest you put your knowledge of body language to the test. The body language of bystanders observing the argument can tell you what the observers believe and whose side they're on. If they've had the opportunity of learning the facts of the case, they'll automatically take sides. When this happens, they'll copy the body language of the person they think is in the right. The more observers there are the better, because they'll unknowingly choose sides. You'll then have a running start on refereeing the argument.

CHAPTER FOUR

DEALING WITH DIFFICULT CLIENTS

GENERAL PRINCIPLES AND TECHNIQUES

For some of us the most difficult and exasperating people we encounter are clients and customers. Companies usually forbid their employees to retaliate when faced with clients' negative behaviour. The result is often frustrated, stressed-out employees.

Those who work on the front lines, representing their company, are susceptible to losing their cool. This is especially true if they have to deal on the phone or in person with angry or dissatisfied clients. Clients who have a beef may be irritable, rude, impatient, persistent, emotional or aggressive. They often choose a representative of the company (possibly *you*) as the butt of their anger. How you handle their problem makes all the difference to how both of you feel. Let's put ourselves in the customer's place for a minute.

Customer Service

Like you and me, customers appreciate courtesy in the service provided to them. One thing employees may forget is that "The customer is always number 1." Some employees give the impression that looking after a client is an interruption to their real work. Such behaviour implies that the employee is doing clients a favour by helping them. In reality, the customer's needs should take precedence over any other work the employee has.

Unfortunately, many people are employed in the service industry simply "because the job was available." These people should be employed elsewhere. If you work in the service industry, ask yourself, "Do I enjoy serving people? Do I want to make their day better than it was before they met me?" If the answer is no — get out of the service industry!

One goal society should have is to create a way of life that allows people to serve others without feeling subservient.

Some men may feel that serving others (either at home or on the job) is demeaning or "women's work." They believe they'll lose their masculinity if they serve others.

Your tone of voice and body language give you away. There's a tremendous difference between starting a conversation with a curt "Yes?" and smiling while saying, "Good morning, how can I help you today?" In a department-store study, I found that six out of ten clerks never smiled. They gave the impression they were doing customers a favour by waiting on them.

Customer service isn't just important for those who work in stores and restaurants. Every kind of organization that exists in society needs proper customer service. Rudeness, impatience and insensitivity aren't compatible with good, professional sales. Even so, salespeople display many of these negative traits for a wide range of reasons. Discourtesy, disrespect, indifference, slow service, ignorance of the services offered by the company, errors and negative behaviour repel customers and leave bad feelings. Customers often respond to the bad feelings by simply staying away.

Customers gravitate to places where they get the most positive feelings. The way employees act with customers is far more important than all the company money spent on advertising and image-building.

How can you improve customer service? If you spend time thinking about ways you can give better service and make customers happier, you'll achieve success wherever you work.

The most successful members of service organizations share common traits. They learn everything they possibly can about their organization and how it can serve its clients better. *Knowledgeable employees know:*

— what their organization does;
— who their key personnel are;

— why the organization works the way it does;
— what service or product the organization offers;
— what common questions or problems are likely to arise;
— how they can help clients most effectively.

Successful employees also manage to find out what customers want, expect and need. They go out of their way to do this by asking questions and really listening to the answers. They anticipate questions about the product or service the company offers.

Do you listen to your customers and honestly try to help them? Keep them informed about what you're doing to meet their needs? Let them know exactly what to anticipate? People almost always accept accurate estimates or honest reasons for delays.

You may think of your job as dull and routine, but you insult your clients if you make them feel as if they're not important or if you look bored with your job. Clients stop buying or switch their buying habits if salespeople don't make the buying experience a pleasant one.

Again trying to put yourself in the customer's place, consider for a moment whether you've encountered the following situations in the past:

- You're five years old, and you've been waiting at the ice cream counter watching much taller people (who came in after you) being served before you.
- You go into a restaurant, sit down and watch others being served. Some people who came in after you are halfway through their meal before your order is taken.
- You go into a department store and stand quietly while the clerks have a little chit-chat before acknowledging you.
- You get gas and have your oil checked. Later you find that the attendant has left oily fingerprints all over your newly washed car.
- You've booked a room, but receive skeptical looks from the front-desk clerk, who can't find your hotel reservation.
- It's raining heavily and you struggle with a rental car released without windshield-washer fluid.
- You order from room service at 7:00 a.m. and have to do without

your breakfast because it doesn't arrive before you have to leave for an 8:30 meeting.

You're short of cash so you write a cheque to yourself. You present it to a teller of your own bank where you're a regular customer. The teller gives you a suspicious look and demands two pieces of personal identification.

I'm sure many of these examples strike a chord with you. Companies should be more aware that a poorly served customer may never come back to use their services. It amuses me to see businesses spending huge sums to get customers back who might never have left if they'd received better service and a little courtesy. That is all your clients expect of you as well.

Real damage is caused when customers storm out of the shop. Not only do many not come back, but they tell all their friends about the poor service, too. If an angry customer comes to you for help, you have the ideal opportunity to prevent that damage. The real disaster hasn't happened yet. If you handle the situation correctly, it *won't* happen. Remember, once you've lost a customer, it's twice as hard to get him or her back.

Have you ever left a store (even though you wanted to buy something) simply because you were not able to get proper service? If customers know they will receive good service, they may be prepared to pay more for an item or accept a substitute for their first choice.

When I'm dissatisfied with service or don't get what I require from a company, I feel I have two choices: (a) I can decide never to go back, or (b) I can give them a second chance.

I've learned to give companies a second chance by complaining to someone who's in a position to correct the situation.

I had received poor service with an airline. Instead of making my travel arrangements with another airline (a definite alternative), I chose to speak to the supervisor of the offending ticket agent. I explained my dilemma to the supervisor, who made the following comment, "If you're happy with our airline — tell everyone. If you're dissatisfied with our service, please tell me — because I'm in a position to do something about it!" He promised to speak to his employee about the problem.

Here are a few situations that may have happened to you. See what you would do:

1. You work for a company that supplies auto parts. You're waiting on clients at the front desk, and a man rushes in. He knows that you're dealing with another customer. He gives the impression that he's in a hurry by shifting his weight from foot to foot, looking at his watch and sighing. How can you make his wait a little easier?

Remember that there's nothing more frustrating than waiting impatiently for a person to assist you who doesn't seem to know you're there. Your first step should be to acknowledge the client's presence. You can do this by saying, "I'll be with you in a moment."

2. You finish with your original client. You nod to the man, and he comes up to the counter. What should you say to him, to make him feel better about having to wait?

Say, "Thank you for your patience. What can I do for you today?"

3. The client shows you a form he has completed that he received in the mail. But someone has sent the wrong order form to him. You explain that it's the wrong form, and he becomes very angry. What should you reply?

Your first impulse might be to say, "Well, I wasn't responsible for sending you the wrong form," (defending yourself), or, "George must have sent it by mistake," (blaming someone else). Would that make him happy? Of course not! He doesn't care who sent him the wrong form, he just wants his car parts!

What you should say is, "I'm sorry you received the wrong form. I don't blame you for being upset, I would be too if that had happened to me. Let me help you fill out the correct form."

In this transaction, you didn't pass the buck. Not only have you apologized for the error and empathized with the person, but you've taken active steps to correct the problem.

4. Suppose it was you who sent the wrong form to him? Do you say, "We've just changed our system, and we don't use that form any more." (passing the buck)? Or do you admit your error? "I'm sorry, I made a mistake. This is the form I should have sent to you. Let me save you some time by helping you fill it out."

Dealing with Frustrated Clients

Here are some of the frustrations (which can lead to anger) clients and customers have identified:

NEED	BLOCK: NO ONE LISTENS TO ME. SOMETHING WENT WRONG. I'M NOT GETTING YOUR HELP. THE PRODUCT DOESN'T WORK.	SATISFACTION OF NEED

Your first step should be to determine what the customer's block is. Then you can concentrate on the problem.

If clients believe that "No one listens to me," and take out their frustration by shouting at you, how can you show them that you're listening? Your body language would show this and you would paraphrase what you believe they have said. Then you would ask questions to learn more about their problem. This would also assist in dealing with "something went wrong," "I'm not getting your help" and "the product doesn't work."

Dealing with Angry Clients

Remind yourself that angry clients probably have a need that isn't being met and believe you have the ability at least to start the problem on the way to being solved. However, you may find it more effective *not* to focus immediately on solving the problem.

First, Deal with the Clients' Feelings. Use empathy — put yourself in their shoes. Say such things as, "I don't blame you for being upset. I'd feel that way too if that had happened to me." Listen carefully, maintaining eye contact, nodding your head, etc. Ask questions to clarify matters for yourself: "And then what happened?" or "Did the item not fit properly?" Then give the client feedback on what you understand the problem (or cause of anger) to be.

Then, Deal with Their Problem. Once you've dealt with clients' feelings, you're now ready to deal with their problem. Find out what they want from you. Say something like, "I see we have a problem here. *What would you like me to do to help you?*" Many employees forget to ask this question, but it is a very powerful problem-solving tool. Often clients don't really know what they want from you. You should then clarify what is really being requested and take steps to solve the problem.

What could you say if you can't do what the person wants? If you just tell someone that you can't meet his or her needs, the person will be understandably unhappy. However, if you can offer alternatives, the person will be less unhappy. Whenever you can't meet a client's needs, tell the person what you *can* do that comes closest to meeting the need. Give the person at least two alternatives, but not more than three. (Any more than three is confusing.) What you've done is return the control of the situation to the client. In the client's mind, he or she is now back in the "driver's seat." The result is a win-win situation.

If there aren't any alternatives, explain the company rules and/or policies that make it impossible to meet the client's request. Explain only what's applicable to the person's own situation. Then work with the client to come up with a course of action (or an alternative you've suggested) so you both understand what's to happen. Make sure you follow up and do what you've said you'll be doing. Give the personal finishing touch (tender loving care) by urging customers to contact you should they have problems in the future.

NOTE: Keep in mind that all problems aren't this easy to solve. You may not be able to satisfy customers fully, but you can try to negotiate with them so there's no winner or loser.

Correcting Your Own Mistakes
What can you do when *you* made the mistake? First, don't be

ashamed to admit it. Then state, "I'm sorry that happened. Let's see what I can do to correct the error." Then correct your mistake. Don't feel you have to defend yourself with such statements as, "We've been frantically busy. That's why I made a mistake." Whatever you do, don't ignore the problem; that will just compound the client's anger at both you and your company.

Do you have a problem admitting that you made a mistake? We all make mistakes, and most of us hate to admit it. But when someone makes a mistake and acknowledges it, doesn't your respect for that person go up? Most people wrongly assume that others will respect them less if they admit to a mistake. The opposite is true. You've blundered, you've admitted it and you're willing to fix the problem. It works far better that way for both of you. If the client continues to argue, say, "What would you like me to do to solve this problem?"

Using the "Stuck-Record" Technique
I have to enforce rules and regulations to my clients. They don't like many of these rules, and I feel pressured when they insist I make exceptions for them.

This is just one of the many problems that are most effectively dealt with by using the "stuck-record" technique.

For example, you could say, "I understand your frustration, but I can't make exceptions for anyone." Or, "I'd like to make an exception in this case, but I can't." If the person continues to complain, calmly repeat exactly what you said before. Repeat it again if the person continues to badger you. Don't raise your voice or get defensive. You'll find that the third time you make the comment, the client will hear you. But remember: when you can't do what a person wants, try to give them at least two alternative solutions if at all possible.

Using the Telephone
If you're like me, and run into someone who doesn't answer the phone properly, your impression of the whole company goes rapidly downhill. Remember, if you answer the phone incorrectly,

you're likely to "turn off" potential and even regular customers.

Creating a favourable impression for your firm is imperative. You may be the first and in some cases the only contact the customer or client has with your firm. Here are some suggestions:

Telephone etiquette

1. Answer calls promptly — on the first ring if possible.
2. Transfer calls effectively. (See "Telephone Responses.")
3. Give progress reports to callers if they're on hold.
4. Never put your hand over the mouthpiece. (The client will think you're being sneaky or that you're talking about them.)
5. No matter how you're feeling at that moment, don't pass your bad mood on to your customer.
6. Keep your cool with difficult customers.
7. *Apologize if you've made a mistake.*
8. Try to give that little extra service to customers that they'll remember for the future.
9. Learn the correct way of making and logging long-distance phone calls.
10. Learn the techniques of feedback and paraphrasing so messages aren't misunderstood.
11. When taking a name, ask the person to spell it for you. Then in brackets, add a phonetic spelling of the name so you won't mispronounce it later.
12. If you leave your work station, make sure you let the receptionist know, or have someone else answer your phone.
13. Keep paper and pen next to *every* telephone.
14. If you must leave the phone to get information, ask whether the caller will wait or will let you call him or her back.
15. If callers ask for information you can't provide, tell them you'll get back to them with the answer. Either return the call yourself, or have someone do it who's more familiar with the subject than you. But make sure someone follows up. The latter suggestion may be preferable when the person may have additional questions during the conversation that you wouldn't be able to answer.
16. Use the caller's name whenever practical (don't overdo this

though). Practise the correct pronunciation of the name.

17. Place long-distance calls yourself. Having your secretary do this often wastes the client's time. This suggests to people that you think their time is less valuable than yours.

18. Have notes ready, related to the call being made, so you won't forget important details. If the call has to be returned, these notes will help you remember everything you wished to discuss.

19. Identify yourself when you answer the phone: e.g., "Bill Baker, Shipping Department."

Remember, you want to be both polite and pleasant, you want the caller to feel important. You want to avoid wasting the caller's time and the company's time. And above all you want to help the caller achieve the purpose of the call.

With a few standard responses you can meet all these goals in most of the situations you will encounter. A number of these standard responses are outlined below.

Telephone responses

Situation	Response
Answering an incoming call.	Accounting Department, Bill Jones speaking.
The person called is on another line.	Mr. Jones is talking on another line. Would you like to hold, or may I ask him to call you?
The person called is away from his or her desk for a few minutes.	Mr. Jones is not in his office right now. May I take a message?
The caller reached the wrong extension.	Our accounting department handles that type of information. May I transfer you?
The person called is in a meeting until 3:00 p.m.	Mr. Jones is attending a meeting until 3:00 p.m. May I ask him to call you?
The person called is with a client.	Mr. Jones is with a client. May I ask him to call you?
The person called has left the office for the afternoon.	Mr. Jones won't be back this afternoon. Would you like him to call you tomorrow?
You need to know who is calling.	May I tell Mr. Jones who's calling please?

The person called is not in yet.	Mr. Jones is not in the office just now. May I ask him to call you? NOTE: Avoid saying, "He hasn't come in yet today," which makes it appear as if he slept in.
The person called is ill.	Mr. Jones isn't in today. May I ask him to call you, or could someone else help you?
You need to give the caller a progress report.	Mr. Jones is still on his line. May I take a message, or ask him to call you?
You are returning to a call on hold.	Thank you for waiting.
The person called is out of town.	Mr. Jones is out of the office until June fourth. May I take a message, or could someone else help you? NOTE: Avoid saying, "He's out of town," which could tell burglars it's safe to break into his home.
You are answering a call transferred to you.	Accounting Department, Bill Jones speaking. May I help you?
The person called is out of the office but will be returning.	Mrs. Jones is away from the office until 2:00 p.m. May I have her call you when she returns? NOTE: Avoid saying, "I have no idea where she is!" (This sounds very unprofessional. You should know where she is!)
The person called is out for coffee.	I expect Mr. Jones in about twenty minutes. May I ask him to call you?
The person called is out for lunch.	I expect Mr. Jones at about 1:00 p.m. May I ask him to call you? NOTE: Don't say he's "Out to lunch," which could mean to some people that he's missing brainpower.
The person called is busy and doesn't want to be disturbed.	Mr. Jones isn't available until 3:00 p.m. Could someone else help you, or may I take a message and have him return your call? NOTE: Saying, "He's tied up right now," brings forth images of someone being tied up with ropes.
You are completing a phone call.	Thank you for calling. Goodbye.
You are placing a call.	Good morning. This is Bill Jones of the XYZ Company calling. May I speak with Mr. Smith, please?

Never give replies like, "She left for lunch about half an hour ago. Call back in two hours, she'll probably be back by then." Or,

"Today's Thursday and she seldom gets in before 10:30 on Thursday." Such replies create a poor impression of the person called and, ultimately, of the company as well.

One answer that covers a multitude of situations is, "I'm sorry, Mr. Jones isn't available right now." Mr. Jones might be sitting right beside you, but he's "not available" to the caller. This makes it unnecessary for receptionists and secretaries to lie for their supervisors. Use this when your supervisor wants you to say, untruthfully, that he or she is not in the office.

Using Common Sense and Good Manners

Here are some situations where good old "common sense" should prevail:

1. Your supervisor has tackled a mountain of work and has left word you're not to disturb him unless the building's on fire. The president of your company phones and asks to speak to your supervisor.

There are exceptions to every rule. This is obviously one of them.

2. You always seem to receive wrong-number phone calls for another firm with a similar phone number.

Don't waste time feeling angry. Instead, look up the number of the company and be ready to give the right number to the caller.

3. Your municipal government department is similar to another department in the federal government. People seem to think you're able to answer their questions.

Have a set spiel explaining the differences in your functions and give callers the correct number. Don't lose your cool — they're not trying to annoy you.

4. You have to escort a visitor from the reception area to your supervisor's office. Do you:
   a. precede the visitor, stating, "Will you follow me, please"?

b. let the visitor go first, stating, "It's down this corridor, first door on your right"?

The correct answer is a.

5. You bring a visitor to your supervisor's office. They've never met before. Do you:
   a. let the visitor walk in?
   b. announce the visitor, saying, "(Supervisor's name), this is Mr. Jones from XYZ Company"?
   c. introduce each to the other?

The correct answer is b.

6. Your supervisor calls you into her office while she has a male visitor. The visitor stands when you enter. Should you:
   a. nod at the visitor, and sit down?
   b. nod at the visitor, and say, "Won't you please be seated?"?
   c. Say, "Hello," and sit down?

Both a and c are correct.

7. Your supervisor's spouse drops in just before closing time. Should you:
   a. call your supervisor on the intercom and follow the instructions given?
   b. offer the visitor a chair in the reception area?
   c. smile and make small talk until your supervisor is available?

The correct answer is a, unless your supervisor is unavailable for a while, then b is correct.

SPECIAL SITUATIONS

Government Offices
Government workers face special problems with clients. Because

governments are not in competition with other firms, the client does not have the option of going elsewhere. As a result, people often go into a government office with a ready-made chip on their shoulder.

Another problem that government workers face is the attitude, "You're working for me. Give me service, or else!" Government employees need to accept that this attitude is common and quite understandable.

These two problems mean that government workers need more empathy and interpersonal skills than other types of employees. Government employers should keep this in mind when hiring staff who deal with the public.

Doctors' Offices

"I work in a doctor's office, and people often call up and want an appointment that day. If I'm booked up, but suggest 10:00 a.m. the next morning, I run into arguments. How can I placate these people and feel less guilty about not being able to help them sooner?"

One reply could be, "I'm sorry Dr. Greg can't see you today. However, I have two vacancies tomorrow morning. Would you prefer a 10:00 a.m. or an 11:30 a.m. appointment?"

Absolve yourself of any guilt this problem generates. If you're doing your job the best way you can, there's no need for you to accept guilty feelings. In the initial situation, when you couldn't conform to the patients' wishes, they likely felt that they had lost control. Giving alternatives will help them regain the feeling that they are in control.

"I'm a receptionist in a doctor's office. Last week, a woman came in with her rowdy two-year-old son. He proceeded to get into everything in the office. I finally picked him up and plunked him on his mother's knee, saying, 'Does this child belong to you? He's getting into things, so you'll have to watch him.' Five minutes later, it was her turn to see the doctor, and she had the nerve to say, 'Look after Johnnie.' I let her know that it wasn't my job to babysit her child. She should have brought someone else to babysit him. I was too busy. She eventually took Johnnie in with her, but she wasn't happy. How could I have handled that situation better?"

This problem occurs in doctors', dentists' and lawyers' offices and it's a serious one. Never pick up children or restrain them unless they're in danger of injuring themselves or others. If you do, the mother could charge you with assault!

Bring the child's disruptive behaviour to the attention of the mother. If the behaviour persists, ask the mother and child to leave. You shouldn't have to babysit, unless there's an emergency of some sort. Keep in mind that, if you agree to care for the child, you may be legally liable should the child be injured while in your care. Check the laws in your area and inform your supervisor of your obligation and liability should you be asked to do this as part of your duties.

Some offices have had to post signs such as: "Your children's behaviour is your responsibility. If they're misbehaving or causing a disturbance, they'll be asked to leave."

Many medical offices have toys for children to play with, but many have signs stating, "These toys are for patients' use only." This discourages parents from using the staff as a babysitter for children who are not there to see the doctor. Again, let your supervisor be your guide on what rules and regulations apply.

"I work in a doctor's office, and callers often refuse to tell me the reason for their appointment. I explain that I need to know so I know how much time to book them for. Their standard answer seems to be, "I only need to see him for five minutes." I then book them in for ten minutes, and find that they need fifteen or twenty because of the complexity of their ailment. If they had explained their ailment to me, I would have known from past patients that they would need that long. Why do patients do this? Do they think I'm being nosy?"

Understand that they may have what they consider a private problem to discuss with the doctor. They may feel that you have no right to know about their innermost secrets. Try using empathy: "I know the matter is personal, but you haven't given me the information I need to set up an appointment." Let them know that you're following the doctor's orders. Use the "stuck-record" method if necessary. Or suggest an alternative, such as, "Would you rather Dr. Smith called you about this matter?"

Restaurants and Hotels

"I work in a restaurant as a waitress. I had a situation the other day that I didn't handle well. There was only one table for two left. First in line was a woman with her son. She explained that it was his birthday, a special occasion for them. They didn't have reservations.

"I was ready to seat them after stating that it was the last table left, when the couple behind her spoke up. 'We have reservations for 7:00. It is now 7:00, and I understand that you have only one table left. My wife and I have to be at a movie at 8:15, so we can't wait until another table's available. We want that one!' They pointed to the last table.

"The woman and the couple argued about who should get the table, and I finally seated the couple with the reservation. The woman and her son became upset and soon left the restaurant before a table was available." ·

There are some situations where "you're damned if you do, and you're damned if you don't." This is one of those situations. Because of the scarcity of tables available, you should have interviewed everyone waiting, to see if there were any who had reservations. The woman and her son would have had to wait for another table. You chose the right solution.

"I'm the registration clerk at a hotel. At 5:00 p.m., a woman came in to register for her room. The hotel was still full from a convention. People were late checking out, so her room wasn't ready. She started running down the hotel, stating what a miserable day she'd been having. The only thing I could suggest was a hospitality suite until hers was ready. She wasn't very happy, but accepted it anyway. What else could I have suggested?"

Find out what extras your hotel offers should this happen in the future. You could have tried the approach of offering alternatives, for instance: "Would you accept the hospitality suite until your room is ready? Or would you rather leave your bags with me and enjoy a complimentary beverage and meal in our restaurant?" (Remember that at 5:00 p.m. she might appreciate refreshments or a meal.) Psychologically this approach puts her back in control because she can choose what she wants to do.

Whenever your company or one of its representatives has caused grief to a client, the client deserves tender, loving care to correct the problem. This T.L.C. can be as simple as solving the problem, or as elaborate as a cash or merchandise bonus. Hotels often give complimentary baskets of fruit or better accommodation if they've caused a client difficulty.

What extras could your company offer to avoid losing the future business of clients who have a legitimate beef?

"I'm a hostess in the banquet room. I was responsible for the comfort and service guests received at a function in the banquet room. The air conditioning wasn't working properly, so we posted NO SMOKING signs throughout the room. The meeting was just going to start when I spotted a man lighting up. I explained about the air conditioning, and asked him to put out his cigarette. He started a disturbance, shouting, 'Discrimination.' I ended up having to call the manager to get him to put it out. What should I have done?"

This man has all the attributes of a "Class Clown." He couldn't help but see the signs, so he knew he was breaking the rules when he lit up. You should have been ready for trouble. I would have told the man that I would like to speak to him outside the room (which removes him from the audience). Then I would have explained the reasons for the NO SMOKING signs.

If he protested, I would have tried the stuck-record technique or given him alternatives. If he wished to smoke, he could do so in the hallway, or in the cafeteria, but not in the banquet room. If he persisted after that point, I would have involved the manager or security officer.

Recreational Facilities
"I work for a recreational facility. I spend most of my day giving people information about public swimming times or ice time. I find this very boring. I also have much more pressing duties to attend to."

Certainly it's not very stimulating giving out the same information over and over again, but have you checked your job description? I bet you'll find that this is the prime function of your position. Repeat calls may be unavoidable, because schedules of recreational facilities change so often. To cut down on many repeat calls, ask clients if they would like to come in and pick up a schedule or offer to mail them one. If you still can't reconcile yourself to this part of your responsibilities, you may have to consider whether you're in the wrong job or are overqualified for the position.

Services to the Elderly
"I have to deal with elderly people. What are some of the things I should remember when dealing with them?"

Sometimes elderly clients can be difficult to deal with. A lot of things are happening to them. Quite often their health isn't as good as it used to be. It's possible their hearing isn't good, or that their thought processes have slowed down a bit.

But imagine how annoying it is to a sprightly eighty-year-old to be yelled at because the speaker assumes all elderly people are deaf. Those who can't hear properly normally have a hearing aid. Don't automatically raise your voice just because a person has white hair.

Again, elderly people may not appreciate being treated as though they're a little simple. Avoid talking down to them. If you're not sure that they have understood, encourage them to paraphrase for you, so you can be sure you have made yourself clear.

Clients with Disabilities
"I sometimes encounter a client who stutters. How should I deal with that problem?"

What errors do you think you commit when in conversation with someone who stutters? Do you finish the sentence for that person? If you finish the sentence incorrectly, this forces the stutterer to start at the beginning again. Can you imagine the double annoyance this is for the person? Stutterers often feel anxiety about being misunderstood. You double their anxiety when you misinterpret what they're going to say by finishing their sentence for them. Have a heart!

Here are a few things to keep in mind when conversing with someone who stutters. Most stutterers are of average or high intelligence. Their brains simply go too fast for their mouths to say what they want to say. Often when they were children, parents and teachers made them self-conscious about their speech, which makes the problem worse.

Start off by letting the stutterer know that you're willing to listen. You do this by using good listening techniques. Give comfortable eye contact, nod your head, ask questions, and by all means let the person finish what he or she is saying. Try to give the impression that you have time for them to say what they want to say. If they try to rush what they're saying, it'll just take longer because of their nervousness.

"I find it difficult dealing with clients who are handicapped. I realize that this is my problem, but what can I do to overcome it?"

The biggest beef handicapped people have against others is that they're treated as nonentities. Do you talk to the companion of the person in the wheelchair, instead of the person in the chair? Many in wheelchairs aren't even given eye contact — in fact most people do anything but give them eye contact. This makes them feel non-existent, and they respond with hostility.

Next time you see someone in a wheelchair, nod or smile and make eye contact. It's better for all concerned if you treat the disabled like everyone else and with respect. Even a severely mentally handicapped person appreciates this.

Offer to help if the person appears to need it. If your offer is rebuffed with a curt, "I can do it myself," don't feel guilty because of the comment. Offer to help, because it may be needed, but respect the person's desire to assert his or her independence and self-sufficiency.

OTHER TYPES OF PROBLEMS

The Client Has Already Had the Run-Around
You answer the phone for your company. The person on the phone is really upset. She has had the proverbial run-around. She says,

"You're the fourth person I've spoken to without getting any answers. Can't anyone help me?"

This person has been the victim of the pass-the-buck syndrome, and the buck should stop with you. Saying, "Sorry, this is the wrong department again," isn't going to be acceptable. She wants her problem solved, and she sees you as being able to help her. She doesn't care if it's "your department" or not. She was frustrated when she first called, but she's now well on her way to becoming very angry. If you also lose your cool and become cross, the problem will get even worse.

Out-of-control anger can be compared to "temporary insanity." If possible, try to prevent your client from becoming temporarily insane, or bring her back to sanity if she's already there. You do this by starting the problem on its way to being solved. If you can do *anything* to move towards a solution, the client will appreciate your help.

This could be done by obtaining all the pertinent information necessary to get the person helped. Then ask for the person's telephone number and have the appropriate employee call her back *within a reasonable length of time!* If the employee can't respond right away, keep the client informed. Give the client your name and number so she can call you back if she doesn't obtain satisfaction from your reference person. Then and only then are you off the hook with the client.

The Client Acts the "Class Clown"

"Class clowns" are difficult to handle. In school, they're the ones who disrupt the class and keep things in an uproar. The aim of this behaviour is to get attention. Children who are class clowns crave any attention they can get and are perfectly willing to accept negative attention rather than have none at all.

How do experienced teachers handle this kind of child? They give the child the attention it craves — but for *good* behaviour. When the child misbehaves, it is isolated from the rest of the class (the opposite of what it wants). Usually the teacher will take the child away from the group and quietly speak to the offender.

When these children become adults, their "class clown" behaviour often continues. They're the people who make sure everyone in the room knows how annoyed they are at something your company has done. They're the ones who want *immediate* attention. If they don't get it, they become verbally abusive and upset everyone around them.

How do you handle these people? The same way you treat children who exhibit this kind of negative behaviour. Take them aside, preferably into a private office. (Don't attempt this if they look physically abusive.) Explain to them that you'll be happy to handle their problem as soon as it's their turn, that if they continue their unacceptable behaviour, you'll be forced to ignore them. Then return them to the area where they were waiting and handle the next customer.

Obviously, before you attempt the above, you should have your supervisor's full approval. If you don't, you may find yourself in the middle if the client decides to go higher with the problem. If you regularly have behaviour problems to deal with, discuss tactics with your supervisor. Review possible strategies and obtain your supervisor's suggestions on how to handle problems. Both of you will then know that difficult situations will be handled consistently.

The Client Refuses to Deal with a Woman

Sally Brown, who's the credit manager for a large construction firm, solved a problem she was facing in a rather humorous way. She had to put up with what seemed like too many clients who insisted on "talking to a man." She solved the problem by patching the calls through to Sam, the janitor in the building. Sam had been clued in and knew how to handle that kind of call. His standard reply was, "I don't know why you're talking to me. Sally Brown's our credit manager. I'll transfer you back to her, and she can look after you."

Another solution would be for Sally to answer her phone by identifying herself clearly. She should say, "Sally Brown, Credit Manager, may I help you?" Most people assume that you're in a low-level position if you answer your phone by just your first name.

Most men answer with full name and title. Women should do the same in order to receive the respect they deserve.

The Client Blames You for Someone Else's Mistake
"I had a problem last week that reduced me to tears. I'm the stockroom clerk in the warehouse of our company. I haven't been on the job for long, and the warehouse manager left me in charge while he picked up some equipment. An angry client phoned in to complain that we had delivered the wrong part and it was costing his company a mint. He called me stupid and acted as if it was all my fault!

"He had ordered the part two months before I even started with the company! I kept insisting that he would have to phone back in fifteen minutes when the warehouse manager returned. I used the "stuck-record" technique, but it didn't seem to work. How should I have handled this irate customer?"

In this case, I can see why the "stuck-record" technique didn't work. You forgot to "turn off" your defence mechanism when the client started yelling at you. What you could have done was take down information as soon as the person started talking. You would have paraphrased and asked questions that would have assisted in solving his problem.

As it was, when the warehouse manager returned fifteen minutes later, no one had started to solve the person's problem. It's likely the manager had to deal with an even angrier client fifteen minutes later! If you had obtained the pertinent information, the warehouse manager would have had some answers for the irate client when he returned his call. Remember this whenever taking a "beef call" for another.

The Client Drops in Without an Appointment
"How should I handle regular clients who just drop in, expecting someone to see them?"

Using the stuck-record technique, tell them, "I'm sorry, you can't see Mr. Jones without an appointment. Would you like to make one for another time?" If the client objects say, "My instructions are that no one's seen unless he or she has an appointment. Would you like to make an appointment for another time?"

The Client Is Long-Winded
"I handle a busy switchboard. When callers want to give me their life story, how can I handle them tactfully?"

Sometimes, it's necessary to interrupt them (they do have to come up for air). Ask if they can *briefly* explain the problem as you'll be passing them on to another person.

"I have a client whom I can't keep on track. He's always going off topic."

When dealing with a compulsive talker, use every conversational gap to guide the conversation towards accomplishing the needs of the phone call. Never show your boredom or frustration, as it'll offend the client. If you give alternatives, the client has to make some decisions. Summarize your conversation, stating what you'll be doing for them, or what they'll be doing for you. Then use this closing clincher: "I believe we've covered everything. I won't take up any more of your valuable time."

The Client Needs an Immediate Answer
"I work in a by-law office, and people phoning in need information immediately. I can't contact the by-law officer because he's out of the office."

One solution is to have a beeper for the by-law officer. Another is to have the officer phone in on a regular basis to obtain messages. Use feedback with the by-law officer to explain the problems you're having with clients and ask his or her assistance in finding solutions.

The Client Is a Know-It-All
"I have trouble dealing with 'know-it-all' people who ask you for information, but really just want to give their own version of what's right."

First — listen to the client's ideas and ask for any facts that support those views. Then, using the information available to *you*, tell the client the real facts. Refer to rules, regulations, policies and procedure manuals or other written data if necessary.

The Client Is Condescending or Rude

"How do I deal with people who are condescending to me — treat me like dirt? They give me the impression that because I'm a clerk I don't know anything. They usually come in to get information regarding college courses."

These are people who probably lack self-assurance and try to put you down to make themselves feel more important. They may or may not use sarcasm to do this. Turn off your defence mechanism. Realize that you are in control of the situation. After all, *they* are coming to *you* for information. Just give them the information they request. Don't allow them to make you lose your cool. You might ask them the show-stopping question, "What do you want me to do to solve this problem?" This often stops them long enough to clarify that they really want from you.

"I've a client who's very rude to me every time he calls in, but is as 'sweet as pie' to my boss. How can I get this person to treat me better?"

Using feedback and the expression, "I have a problem, and I need your help in solving it . . . ," explain to your supervisor the rudeness of this client. Ask your supervisor to speak to this person about the matter. The client should know that this is unacceptable behaviour to any employee of the company. If your supervisor won't back you up, transfer this person's call directly to the supervisor without having any further exchange with that person.

The Client Puts Your Long-Distance Call on Hold

"When I call long distance, I get furious if the receptionist puts me on hold without asking whether I object. How can I deal with being put on 'ignore' in the future?"

If this is a regular occurrence, talk to the receptionist's supervisor and explain the inconvenience and costs this delay gives you. I jump right in and say that my call is long-distance even before identifying whom I am calling. I say, "Long distance for Marie Baker." They assume I'm a long-distance operator and put the call through right away. A more drastic solution is to bill this client for the time you were put on hold.

You Have to Deal with Two Clients Simultaneously
"I never know whether I should handle the person on the phone or the person who has waited to see me for fifteen minutes. Who should get priority?"

Answer the phone and tell the caller you're with a client and will be a few minutes. Give alternatives. Ask whether the caller would like to call back, have you return the call later or be put on hold. Then alternate between those who have come in in person and those who phone in.

"I work for a parts department of an auto-supply firm. I'm trying to get them to set up a numbering system, so customers are dealt with in turn. Right now, because it's hard to keep track of who is next (I have to go into the warehouse to get their parts) I often can't be sure in what order to help people. I've had to referee several battles about whose turn it is, and I find that it gets me rattled."

After you decided whom you would serve first and had eventually dealt with the two irate customers, you should have reminded yourself, "That was certainly an unpleasant encounter, but I did the best I could." Remember, in situations like this, no matter whom you serve first, you're "damned if you do and damned if you don't." You have no reason to take on guilt feelings because you couldn't please them both simultaneously. Use feedback with your supervisor to explain the difficulties not having a numbering system is causing you and the rest of the staff. (You could also try setting up an informal numbering system on your own, while you wait for the firm to act.)

The Client Refuses to Wait His or Her Turn
"My boss, a lawyer, is very busy. Last week a friend of his needed some

legal advice and expected service immediately. I explained the situation and suggested that he make an appointment. The friend barged right past me into my boss's office, where he was in a meeting with a client. How could I have handled that situation better?"

Talk to your supervisor and ask him what you should do if a similar situation happens in the future. Unless you had used some fast judo or karate, the friend would have been in your supervisor's office before you could react anyway. Throw your guilt trip out the window. At the time you did the best you could to handle the situation.

The Client Uses Profane Language or Threatening Behaviour

"What should I do when my caller uses profane language on the phone? Do I have to put up with that kind of garbage?"

I don't believe anyone should have to put up with profane language. You should be able to hang up on the caller. Check with your supervisor to see what you're expected to do. It's possible, because of the work you do, that you do have to put up with that kind of garbage — for instance, if you're working in an emergency ward of a hospital. It's part of the pattern for some people to start swearing when upset about something. You can't just refuse to handle the problem of this upset person. If you're working on a crisis or emergency line of any kind, you have to know that this language may go with the territory. You may, however, ask such callers to clean up their language so you can handle their difficulty better. But above all, make sure you know what your supervisor wants you to do.

"How about drunk or threatening people?"

Another topic that you must talk about to your supervisor *before* it happens. Know when to call in a security guard or the police. Knowing what steps to take and having an emergency plan of your own makes you more confident when having to deal with such unexpected and unsettling problems.

CHAPTER
FIVE

DEALING WITH DIFFICULT SUPERVISORS

If you're not enjoying your work, there could be a number of reasons why. One possible cause of job dissatisfaction is poor supervision. Some individuals have been chosen for their supervisory positions because they know a lot about the type of work done by those they are supervising. They may know next to nothing, however, about how to motivate *people*.

If you think your supervisor's "style" of managing is responsible for your job dissatisfaction, this chapter is for you.

POOR MOTIVATORS

Many employees are self-motivating and will work well even under poor supervision. Every employee, however, can respond to and benefit from a supervisor who understands what motivates people to do their best work. Because not every employee is the same, a good supervisor will develop insight into which employees respond best to praise, which to monetary incentives and which to opportunities to learn new things or to prepare for promotion.

If your motivation at work is suffering, it may be because your supervisor doesn't understand that some or all of the following working conditions can have a powerfully *de*motivating effect.

1. *Restrictive supervision.* You'll likely obtain less job satisfaction if your supervisor gives you little chance to take an active part in how you complete your assignments. The more employees parti-

cipate in how they do things, the more co-operative they will be.

Supervisors who use an authoritarian leadership style are setting themselves up to fail. If you have this type of supervisor, try feedback to alleviate the problem. If your supervisor won't be reasonable and you can't change his or her behaviour, you may have to suffer for a while until a promotion is available. Alternatively, you could take a lateral move to another department or, as a last resort, leave the company you're with.

2. Lack of recognition. Supervisors demotivate staff if they identify only what their subordinates have done wrong. They should concentrate instead on what they have done right, to encourage better performance.

In the old school of management, supervisors believed it was their right to take credit for new ideas suggested by their subordinates. As you might expect, this just demotivates employees, discourages new ideas and perpetuates mediocre performance and marginal productivity. Progressive supervisors are learning that if they give employees credit where credit is due, their staff is motivated to perform better. Employees whose supervisors are still stingy with recognition could try using feedback to alleviate this problem. Possibly, the supervisor isn't aware of how demotivating his or her actions are. Say, "I have a problem, and I need your help in solving it. In the past week I've gone out of my way to do an exceptional job on the Miller project and have worked overtime to meet the deadline. I'm discouraged because all I've heard about the project is the 2 per cent I did wrong. What about the 98 per cent I did right? It's not very encouraging to hear only the negatives. Do you understand what I mean?"

This should help the supervisor do a better job in future by giving positive reinforcement when it's due.

3. Monotonous work. Some companies implement job rotation for employees in an attempt to make employees' jobs more interesting. Job rotation is possible if there are several employees in a company who work at substantially the same class or level of work and in the same pay range. Employers and employees alike benefit from job rotation, because staff members can fill more than one job and the work of absent employees can be done by someone else. If your company is doing this, management is trying to keep your work interesting. If they haven't tried job rotation, suggest they do so, for all your sakes!

4. *Little opportunity to try new ideas.* Employee motivation also suffers when supervisors ignore workers' suggestions for better ways of doing their jobs. Because the employees are doing the actual work, they are often in the best position to come up with better and quicker ways to do the job.

If your supervisor is weak in this area, plant seeds for change slowly. Let him or her get used to a new idea gradually. Use facts to back up your suggestions, and identify any cost reduction that can be achieved by doing it the new way. Be open, however, to legitimate reasons why your idea won't work. If your supervisor won't respond to any suggestions, use feedback to describe your frustration.

5. *No opportunities to acquire new skills.* At one time, companies spent many training pounds on their employees and still couldn't keep up with the demand for competent qualified people. Recently, companies have had to tighten their training budgets. Companies may refuse to give training that they believe employees can't use right away. Employees whose promotions are six months to one year away may find it difficult to obtain training.

To be sure they are ready for the next step up, employees who find themselves in this position would be wise to obtain and pay for this training themselves. The employee thus gains an edge over others who have not acquired the necessary skills. Money spent on training is a good investment by the employee.

6. *Absence of job descriptions and performance appraisals.* Companies that practise good management systems know that both accurate, up-to-date job descriptions and performance appraisals are essential for high productivity and motivation of staff. When staff know what's expected of them, they perform better.

If more than 5 per cent of your duties fit into the category "other duties as assigned," your job description isn't accurate. How do you go about getting a more realistic one?

You could simply itemize your duties and the percentage of your time spent on each item. Your request for reclassification will be based on factual information. Or, if your job description is more than two years old, it's probably outdated. Again, you need to itemize your duties and the percentage of your time each takes, before pointing out discrepancies between your job description and your actual job and asking for reclassification. A good time to ask for a job-description update is when you have your yearly performance appraisal.

What if tasks are regularly added to your duties without any reclassification of your position? If you are always being given more of the *same* kind of task (job dumping), you can't request a reclassification. But if your new tasks have a different level of responsibility, then your job probably should be reclassified. You would need to use facts to prove that your responsibility level had changed.

In large companies, there are usually formal classification systems. If you work for a small company, you might have some difficulty. Job classification is based on the responsibility level of the tasks performed by the person in the position. If the level of responsibility changes, either upward or downward, the position is usually reclassified. For example, a secretary whose supervisor takes on extra responsibilities will most likely need a job reclassification, because the responsibility level of the secretary rises with the supervisor's. On the other hand, if the supervisor's position is abolished, and the secretary now works for four lower-level people, the responsibility level of the job will be lower, and the position could be reclassified to a lower level.

What if your employer says, "We don't have job descriptions here"? In that case, you should write one yourself (using examples found at the library, or accurate descriptions of a friend's position as a guideline). Take it to your supervisor and ask for approval. If approval is refused, ask, "How can I do a good job for you, if neither of us knows what I'm supposed to do?"

7. *Discrepancy between pay and level of responsibility.* If you're convinced that your salary level is too low for the kind of work you're doing, you'll have to look at your current job description, make any changes necessary, then ask for an appointment with your supervisor. At the meeting, explain that your duties are listed incorrectly and that you have much more responsibility than the description shows. Or perhaps your job description is accurate, but the salary range for it doesn't reflect the job's importance to the company. Find out what similar positions are earning in competitive companies. Expressions such as, "I think I'm underpaid," will not help you; go in equipped with *facts*. You must be able to give reasons to back up your request for more money. If this fails, you may have to leave the company you're with and look elsewhere.

8. *Unpaid overtime.* In some areas, an employer has the choice of either paying employees for overtime or giving them time off in lieu of overtime pay. This is usually dependent on the terms of your contract with your company. Check with your employer whether overtime is paid and at what rate when you first join. Overtime policy varies from company to company.

THE AGGRESSIVE SUPERVISOR
In an ideal world all supervisors would be assertive (rather than passive or aggressive), pleasant, supportive, efficient, tactful and blessed with superior insight into human nature. In the real world, however, supervisors display the usual range of human faults and failings. Supervisors who use aggressive behaviour to dominate and control their staff are among the most difficult for an employee to deal with.

Aggressive supervisors haven't learned one of the fundamentals of good supervision. Employees can't be forced into doing a good job, they're led into it. Supervisors are bound to receive poor productivity from their staff if they:

— discipline employees publicly;
— bully them into working excessively long hours;
— are hypercritical and impossible to please;
— criticize individuals rather than behaviour.

Before you decide to say anything to an aggressive supervisor, ask yourself if you might make matters worse by saying something. If this person treats *everyone* the same belligerent way, it may not be worth the risk of discussing the matter. You may have to mark time until you can get away from this bully.

If you decide it might help to discuss the problem, use feedback to let your supervisor know how his or her behaviour is affecting you. This takes courage, but at least you will know you made an effort to improve matters. Talk to your supervisor privately about his or her aggressive behaviour. If the problem is "labelling," for example, say, "I have a problem and I need your help in solving it. I find it difficult to handle the put-downs you've been giving me lately. I can't defend my actions when you call me names. The way it is now, I don't know how to improve my performance or what you really want of me. Could you give me examples of why you think I'm ignorant?"

If the situation doesn't change, don't go higher up to his or her supervisor to complain. Instead:

— put up with it as long as you can, then ask for a transfer to another position in the company;
— talk to someone in your personnel department; or
— leave for greener pastures elsewhere.

Go higher up the chain of command only when the supervisor's behaviour is affecting the rest of the staff. Only group complaints can oust a bad supervisor and then only if the complaint is handled correctly. Make sure the group uses facts to explain its grievances. Have details of what has actually happened, costs in pounds, damage to customer relations, delays, unmet deadlines, unnecessary overtime, production stoppages, etc.

When you feel your supervisor has removed all the pride and pleasure you obtain from your work, then it's time to leave.

As we have seen, aggressive behaviour can take a variety of forms. Ways of dealing with some of these are worth discussing in detail.

1. **Sarcasm.** Some sarcasm is nothing more than harmless kidding. It is non-threatening and can be fun. However, sarcasm can also be hurtful, designed to make others feel small. People using it

feel a sense of power at seeing other people squirm. Hurtful sarcasm is a form of indirect aggression — one of the sneakiest, most manipulative and underhanded methods of getting your way.

People who use hurtful sarcasm often don't feel very good about themselves, so they attempt to put others down to make themselves feel more important. The game continues when others respond defensively or act hurt. Sarcastic people want others to get angry and defend themselves. Remind yourself not to respond negatively to their remarks. Try to stick to the facts.

Think for a minute: who's in control in the situation when sarcasm is used? You are (the recipient of the sarcasm) until you reply. Should you respond to sarcasm with more sarcasm? No — if you do, you often just encourage more of the same. Instead, try to analyse why the person might feel the need to put you down. Once you have an idea of what really prompts the sarcasm, you'll be able to deal with the actual issue.

Don't react to sarcasm — turn it off. The sarcastic person won't know what to do, because you're not playing by "the rules." When it's no longer fun to throw things at you, the culprit will take his or her sarcastic remarks elsewhere.

If you can't stay quiet, and you feel that the sarcasm warrants a response, you might say, "Your last comment was very sarcastic, and a put-down. Put-downs hurt. Can you explain why you said what you did?" Or, "Why do you feel you have to give me a put-down like that?" Or, "That was pretty sarcastic. What is it that you really want to say to me that you're covering up with sarcasm?" Make aggressive people account for their actions. Often they aren't aware of how destructive their behaviour is to others.

When I was doing the research for my first book, *Escaping the Pink-Collar Ghetto*, I interviewed more than 700 managers (695 of them men) to see why they weren't promoting more women. Initially, I was met with a crossed-arms defensive stance from most of the managers. I knew they were on the defensive when the sarcasm started to flow. My instinctive reaction was to fight sarcasm with sarcasm, but instead, I stood back from the situation and tried to analyse it. I concluded that these managers felt that when I asked, "Why aren't you promoting more women?" I was accusing them of discriminatory behaviour.

I reassured them by explaining fully what I was there to accomplish: that I really needed their input to find out what mistakes women were making that kept them from being promoted. I gave several examples other companies had given me and asked them if the same was true in their company as well. Soon they realized that I was there only to obtain information and their help, not to push them into defending the scarcity of women in senior positions in their company. Most were then very co-operative.

They would not have been, however, if I had responded defensively to their sarcasm.

2. *Ignoring, or the silent treatment.* Another form of indirect aggression is ignoring others or giving them the silent treatment, by refusing to discuss important issues with them. Some supervisors even refuse to speak to a staff member about anything for days even though they're members of the same department! This is cruel and almost as destructive as vindictive sarcasm.

This negative action is a no-win situation for both parties involved. Often the person giving the silent treatment wins the battle, but prolongs the war. If issues are not settled through discussion, they will inevitably resurface later.

Brian felt proud when his department head commended him in front of his co-workers and supervisor for the excellent job he had done on a project. Brian had worked hard to complete the project and felt he deserved the praise. Later that day, he asked his supervisor, Harry, for technical advice relating to his newest project. Harry was very abrupt, and told him to figure it out himself. During the next week, Brian received the "cold shoulder" from Harry, who wasn't as available or supportive as usual. Brian decided to speak to Harry. He said, "I have a problem and I need your help in solving it." He used feedback to explain how he felt when Harry withdrew his help, and asked him to explain why this was happening.

Harry admitted that he was upset when Brian received praise from the department head, and that he felt jealous because this had never happened to him in the past. He promised to be more available in the future.

3. *Tantrums.*
"How do I deal with my boss? He has tantrums on a regular basis. He slams down the phone, bangs his desk drawers, throws things and slams his office door. I'm completely unnerved by his behaviour and became very shaky and nervous. What should I do when this happens in the future?"

People who still resort to temper tantrums as adults haven't completely grown up. A friend advised this employee to picture her boss wearing a bonnet and nappy, sitting in a high chair, banging a spoon on the tray.

She used this stress reliever the next time he had a tantrum and found that bringing forth this humorous mental image kept her from losing her cool with him. She even had the courage one day (after he had settled down) to ask, "Are you finished?"

"Finished what?" he thundered.

"I wondered if you were finished having your temper tantrum?"

He sat quietly for a minute, smiled sheepishly and said, "I guess that's what you would call it, wouldn't you? Yes, I've finished having my temper tantrum."

She did the same thing the next time he had a tantrum, with the same smiling reaction, until finally she didn't have to say anything. He would come to his office door and say, "It's okay now — I'm finished." The beautiful spin-off of this situation was that he soon stopped having tantrums entirely.

Humour can get you through many difficult situations. The above example shows that humour can diffuse anger. Somehow, when we're able to laugh about something, the tension lessens. Use funny mental pictures or even place a favourite cartoon near your desk to remind you to see the funny side of situations.

4. *Sexual harassment.*
Sexual harassment is usually thought of as a problem for women in the work place, but men also have unwanted sexual advances directed at them.

This work problem has been affecting employees for centuries. Laws pertaining to harassment are changing rapidly. Whether you're a man or a woman, I urge you to investigate relevant legislation. Learn about sexual harassment, and how you can reduce it or deal with it. (See the Appendix for where to go for help with sexual harassment.) Research shows that 70 to 80 per cent of women in America have experienced one or more forms of sexual harassment by superiors or co-workers. Fifty-two per cent of them lost or left a job because of it.

The following types of behaviour can all be regarded as sexual harassment:

— unwelcome sexual remarks such as jokes, innuendo, teasing and verbal abuse;
— taunts about a person's body, attire, age, marital status;
— displays of pornographic or offensive pictures;
— practical jokes that cause awkwardness or embarrassment;
— unwelcome invitations or requests, whether indirect or explicit;
— intimidation;
— leering or other suggestive gestures;
— condescending or paternalistic treatment that undermines self-respect;
— unnecessary physical contact, such as touching, patting, pinching, punching or physical assault.

A related problem is a type of reverse discrimination that occurs when promotions and bonuses are awarded to an employee in return for sexual favours, while other employees who have earned recognition through good work are passed over.

If you are the object of sexual harassment you should:

1. Tell the person that you object to whatever he or she is doing or saying. Let him or her know you really mean it! If necessary, explain that this behaviour could be classified as sexual harassment and you expect it to stop immediately. Have a friend with you for support and/or as a future witness. If you feel unable to tackle the harasser yourself, ask a personnel officer or your trade union representative to approach them on your behalf. Keep a written record of occasions when harassment occurs – you may have to recall specific details in the event of an enquiry or subsequent Industrial Tribunal hear-

ing. Your record should include dates, times, names of witnesses, etc.

2. If the harassment occurs again, repeat your earlier objections. Back them up with a written letter or memo. Refer to your earlier spoken complaint. State only the facts. Make *at least three copies* of this letter. Send one copy to the offending person and one to his or her supervisor. Keep one copy for your records. Report the harassment to management and/or institute the grievance procedure if there is one. Every incident is worth reporting and any form of assault should be reported to the police without delay.

3. Confide in colleagues; it may be that others are suffering too. This can often be a valuable source of support.

4. Keep a record of what management does to investigate your complaint. Also record meetings and hearings in connection to the matter. Ask for details of what the investigation decided and recommended. If your harasser begins to ignore you, pass your work to others or other such tactics, report this immediately.

5. If the behaviour continues, or the company fails to deal with it to your satisfaction, go to your union. You can contact a national officer or the union's women's officer, if appropriate, if your local official is not forthcoming. You can also approach the Equal Opportunities Commission for further advice. It is important to remember that there is a three month time limit for taking cases to the Industrial Tribunal.

No longer can others in positions of power look the other way and ignore the fact that sexual harassment is occurring. A supervisor who does nothing about the sexual harassment of an employee is regarded as having condoned the harassment. If the employee knows that the supervisor has observed or is aware of the situation, he or she can include the supervisor in the charge of sexual harassment.

SUPERVISORS WITH DEFICIENT SUPERVISORY SKILLS

Many supervisors, unfortunately, have had little or no supervisory training. Everyone benefits from this kind of training. Even if supervisors have to pay for the training themselves, it's one of the best investments they can make towards their future success.

Supervisors who lack supervisory training can be very frustrating to work for. They may not know how to delegate, how to discipline subordinates, or how to motivate different types of employees. Or, in various ways, they may make it difficult for their staff to operate efficiently. If your supervisor is one of these, you may have to take active steps and suggest the company provide him or her with supervisory training.

1. *Poor delegation*
"My boss is great with people, but is vague at times on how he wants me to do things. He gives unclear directions, then changes his mind the next day."

You'll succeed with this type of boss if you fill in the details of any work he delegates to you. Use paraphrasing to make sure that what he originally says is what you actually hear. If there are any unclear areas, ask questions about what he wants. If he's in the habit of changing his mind the next day, write down the instructions, show the list to him, and confirm his instructions.

Later, show your confusion when he changes his instructions and bring out your list of instructions made earlier. Update the instructions as requested. Soon your supervisor will realize how often he changes his instructions. He may learn to take more time when formulating his requests. This person would probably benefit greatly by attending a time-management course. This would teach him to save time by planning before delegating tasks to subordinates.

Sometimes supervisors are disorganized. They're the ones that explain that they know where everything is on their messy desks. They hate details. This boss hates bad news, so stress what you're going to do about things, rather than dwell on the problem.

"My boss asks me to do things that really aren't my job."

Use paraphrasing to make sure you understand what your supervisor expects from you. Have your job description updated. Then talk with your supervisor to see if someone else can handle a duty that you feel doesn't fit your position.

DIFFICULT SUPERVISORS 119

2. *Obsessive perfectionism*
"My boss is a perfectionist who sometimes expects too much from his staff."

Anticipate your boss's needs. Don't skip details. Give alternatives. Have plans B and C available, should they be necessary. Submit new ideas in writing, including the pros and cons and the alternatives available.

3. *Poor disciplinary technique*
"My boss disciplines me in public."

This is a major *faux pas* on the part of your supervisor. Your first attempt should be to make the person understand and empathize with your feelings. Use the technique of feedback to let the supervisor know how humiliating it is when he or she disciplines you in front of others. Explain that you could accept criticism far more easily if it were given privately. You might have to add, that if you are publicly disciplined in future, you'll simply walk away.

4. *Over-orientation towards competition*
"My boss is a very competition-oriented person. He wants me to compete with co-workers and I don't want to."

You may be in the wrong profession. Competing against other employees is the most popular system management uses to encourage staff to make more sales.

Many people respond much better to the challenge of beating their own sales records than to competition with others. Companies should ensure that the standards of competition are fair to those at all levels of experience. If you're new with the company, you can't be expected to compete with someone with an established territory and clientele. Trainees with six months' experience should compete against others in the company with the same experience. Many in sales enjoy competition. Others don't, but are encouraged to set realistic objectives for themselves.

Many sales supervisors can be very stressful to work for. They expect assertive or aggressive behaviour from their staff. Pushover behaviour is not acceptable. You need to prepare carefully to discuss a problem with such a boss. Be sure you have several workable solutions to suggest before attempting to negotiate changes.

5. *Failure to back up staff*
"My boss doesn't back me up when I get into trouble with clients. She always takes the client's side, and I end up defending myself, even though I'm in the right."

Supervisors who automatically take the client's side in a client-employee dispute are doing their subordinates a grave injustice. Until the employee has had a chance to explain his or her side of the story, the supervisor should remain neutral.

The supervisor should record all the facts given by the client and assure the client that the matter will be investigated.

If your supervisor fails to back you up when you know you're carrying out your duties correctly, use the feedback technique to explain how you feel about being unjustly blamed.

Say, "I have a problem and I need your help in solving it. Last week Mrs. Smith wanted me to bend the rules for her. I explained to her that I had strict guidelines I was expected to follow and said I couldn't do what she wanted. She then spoke to you and got her way. This same thing has happened with four clients in the past month. I felt pretty foolish when she came by my office to tell me she had got what she wanted. I'm wondering if the rules have changed and how I'm to deal with these kinds of problems in the future."

6. *Failure to give credit for special contributions.* I've heard both
women and men say (and we'll assume the boss is a man), "I worked all week on that report, and my boss took full credit for it. That's the last time he's going to do that to me!"

When your supervisor "steals" your ideas and takes credit for them, you've made him look good. He needs you to do this. If you don't let him take the credit, he'll hold you back.

For instance, if you write a new policy-and-procedures manual for your department, your supervisor can take full credit for its contents. He has the right (according to the existing rules of business) to use your ideas, and do it with a clear conscience.

According to business rules, you (the subordinate) are there to make your supervisor or manager look good. Your ideas become your supervisor's ideas, and the supervisor is not breaking any rules by taking the credit. Most men and women dislike this rule. Many supervisors don't feel that they're doing anything wrong, because "everybody does it."

I disagree completely with this business practice, and encourage supervisors to give credit where credit's due. Supervisors who keep stealing their subordinates' ideas only demotivate them. Chances are, they'll get bad suggestions or no suggestions at all from their staff in the future. If a subordinate has come up with a new method of making a widget, that employee should get the praise and recognition, not the supervisor. What does it matter if the subordinate gets the credit for the good idea? The supervisor could submit the report under his or her name, but give credit to the subordinates who helped prepare the report.

If your supervisor is an old-style limelight-stealer and you can't go along with it, send your new ideas or suggestions to him or her in the form of a memo. Ask for your supervisor's opinion about the merit of your idea. Then it's in writing. Or offer your suggestions at a meeting where others know that it's *your* idea.

"I have to do my boss's work in an acting capacity without extra pay. When he's away, I have to handle his job as well as my own. I don't think this is fair."

Try using the feedback technique to explain your problem. If that doesn't work, look upon the experience as a developmental phase of your employment. Ask your supervisor which duties you can let slide during this double-duty period.

It looks excellent on a résumé when you're able to add "acting supervisory duties while supervisor away." This statement may help you get future supervisory positions. So take the extra work anyway, if you think you can manage to handle two jobs for short periods.

7. **Interference.** Dennis had a problem with his manager, Jim. Dennis was new in his position as supervisor of a staff of four. Under

the guise of "helping" him, Jim allowed Dennis's staff to bypass Dennis to obtain help directly from him.

Jim was breaking one of the cardinal rules in business by undermining the control and authority Dennis needed to supervise his staff properly. There's a strict rule in business regarding the line of command: managers are not supposed to bypass a supervisor to give work directly to the supervisor's subordinates. Nor should managers get involved in matters of discipline or in performance appraisals that concern the supervisor's staff. Dennis was advised to use the feedback technique to explain that his group's effectiveness was undermined when he had only partial control over his subordinates' work. He should remind Jim that he, Dennis, is ultimately responsible for everything he and his staff do and that he needs full control to do his job effectively.

8. *Unavailability to staff and clients.* Shirley asked how she could get her supervisor to tell her where he was. There was an in-out board, but he seldom used it and often left by the back door. He was seldom available: was either in meetings, out of the office, or sitting behind a closed door.

Shirley was advised to itemize occasions when she had been forced to handle problems on her own and to give her supervisor a list of the difficulties that arose because he wasn't available for consultation. She should then ask her supervisor if there is an alternative supervisor she could consult when he can't be reached.

9. *Failure to respect employees' privacy*
"My supervisor wants to know all about my personal life and I don't want to talk about it."

Say, "I prefer to keep a clear division between my private and business life. I've found it's better for me." If your supervisor pushes further, ask, "Why is my private life so important to you?" The supervisor is thus forced to account for his or her aggressive behaviour.

10. *Failure to provide opportunities for growth.* Peter felt frustrated because his supervisor refused to give him assignments that would prepare him for his next promotional opportunity. His title was Buyer 1 (the first step on the ladder for the purchasing manager's position). His supervisor, Mel, had been in the Buyer 2 position for five years. He refused to allow Peter to learn anything relating to a future promotion.

In this situation, Mel felt Peter was a "heel-nipper" (someone after his supervisory job), while Peter felt that Mel was "locked into" his position and threatened by Peter's promotional expectations.

Mel didn't understand that his reluctance to prepare Peter for his position was why he wasn't moving ahead in the company. Often, supervisors who have no one ready to take over their position will themselves be overlooked for a promotion. Peter was advised to bring this information to Mel's attention. If that didn't work, he could take a lateral move into a position comparable to his existing one, or try for a promotion in another department.

He was initially reluctant to move to another department because such a move represented a detour from the direct route to the purchasing manager's position. When I explained that this might be the only way he could bypass Mel's position, he agreed to try it. He's now the purchasing manager, and supervises Mel.

THE GENTLE ART OF BEING SUPERVISED

An important factor affecting your dealings with your supervisor is your own attitude to supervision. Even the best employees sometimes need guidance and even correction from their supervisor. It is true that there are difficult supervisors who habitually give the necessary guidance in negative form, as criticism. But there are also employees who are too ready to perceive legitimate correction as criticism.

The art of being supervised consists of being able to accept suggestions that will help you improve your performance. Whether these suggestions come to you in the harsh form of criticism or in the milder form of correction or instruction, you need to learn how to handle them in a positive way. The following steps may help you in your effort to learn the delicate art of being supervised.

When your supervisor corrects or criticizes you:

1. Control your thoughts and behaviour. Keep in mind that there may be some truth in the criticism (you'll miss it if you concentrate only on how you can defend yourself).
2. Don't respond angrily. Instead, listen carefully to the comments.
3. Ask for specifics if the criticism is vague. For example, if your supervisor says, "I don't like your attitude," ask "What is it about my attitude that concerns you?" Your supervisor might respond with, "Well, you were rude to Mrs. Smith when you served her a few minutes ago. You kept her waiting far too long before you looked after her." You may not like what you hear, but at least now you have something specific to deal with.
4. Use the technique of paraphrasing to confirm your understanding of the problem.
5. If the criticism is valid, apologize and let your supervisor know what steps you'll take to correct the behaviour or the problem. Leave guilt trips behind. Don't let the criticism overwhelm you and affect the rest of your day; instead, simply decide that you won't make the same mistake again.
6. Above all, don't climb into a shell, work to rule or give poor performance should you be criticized for something. We often set up this kind of defence mechanism in ourselves. If we feel that something or someone hurts us (especially a supervisor), we're likely to back off and "lick our wounds."

CHAPTER SIX

DEALING WITH DIFFICULT CO-WORKERS

In a sense everyone employed by your company is your co-worker, but for the purposes of this chapter, "co-worker" refers to employees whose behaviour in the work place affects you, but with whom you have no direct reporting relationship (they do not supervise you; you do not supervise them).

Dealing with difficult co-workers can be tricky, because if you try to get them to change their behaviour and don't handle it just right, they may think you're trying to "boss" them. And "bossing" co-workers when you're not their supervisor is, of course, a classic work place no-no.

As with other groups of difficult people, co-workers' difficult behaviour takes a variety of forms.

UNPROFESSIONAL BEHAVIOUR
Most employees want to do a good job, and to be important to their companies. People who are committed to doing the best job possible set high standards for their own job performance and earn the right to be very proud of their work. Their consistently professional behaviour also brings them the trust and respect of supervisors, clients and co-workers.

The professionalism of your colleagues will, to a large extent, determine whether your work place is congenial or not. In most work places, people's jobs are interdependent, and each worker's effectiveness and productivity is usually tied in some way to how well others perform their roles in the company. The unprofessional behaviour of one employee can affect the efficiency of many. Although most of us would prefer to live and let live, when a co-worker's inefficiency interferes with our own performance, it is useful to know what sort of action can be taken to correct the problem.

1. *Shirkers.*   Do you have co-workers who don't do their share of the work, but receive more than their share of salary? If you feel this is true, discuss it with your boss. Companies that implement a "merit system" fairly, seldom face this problem.

People may use a variety of tactics to avoid their responsibilities. Being habitually late and being away from their desks are two of the commonest ploys. There are three kinds of time watchers. Let's say all three types have a 10:00 a.m. appointment.

Type 1 people arrive right on the dot of 10:00.
Type 2 people arrive at 10:10 and fully believe they're on time.
Type 3 people arrive at 9:50 and feel they've "just made it!"

Type 2 time-users assume that other people don't mind waiting. This false belief has kept many a person from obtaining a sale, closing a deal and obtaining a contract. People don't like to be kept waiting! They feel that their time is important — and object to being treated as if it isn't.

"I have a friend that I often have lunch with or attend meetings with, but she's always late! Besides using feedback, what else can I do to solve this situation?"

Let her know what the consequences will be should she keep you waiting the next time. Tell her that if she isn't ready when you come for her, you'll leave without her. Then do it! If you are to meet her for lunch, wait only ten minutes before ordering your meal.

George works at a front desk of a government office, and deals directly with the public. Bill, a co-worker, is often late for work. This makes George's job twice as busy, because he has to cover the desk by himself.

Using feedback he said, "Bill, you probably don't realize the double workload I have every time you're late. This makes our department look bad. What do you think you can do to stop this from happening in the future?" (Note that George focused on the consequences for the department, not any personal grievance he felt.)

1. The problem — George has a double workload when Bill is late for work.
2. George's stated feelings or reaction — This makes their department look bad.
3. The solution — George asked Bill to solve the problem.

Betty is a receptionist. One of her duties is to answer the phone for her department. They have in-out boards that all members of the staff are supposed to keep up to date. Unfortunately, one employee, Mildred, leaves her desk, and even the office, without telling Betty where to find her. Nor does she have someone else answer her phone for her when she isn't able to. When clients ask for Mildred, Betty puts the caller through to her desk. If Mildred doesn't answer after the first few rings, the call is returned to her.

Betty said she felt like a fool when she had to explain that she didn't know where Mildred was, or when she would return.

Using feedback, she started the conversation by saying, "I have a problem and I need your help in solving it." Then she asked Mildred what she would suggest to stop the problem from recurring. (This dumps the problem into Mildred's lap where it belongs.) Mildred still shrugged it off, so Betty added, "I need your co-operation so I can do my job properly for the company. It must appear pretty tacky to the client when I have to admit that I don't know where you are. Can we find some solution that will be acceptable to both of us?"

Betty's persistence eventually produced a compromise that was acceptable to both women. Mildred agreed that she would let Betty know where she was. She arranged for a co-worker to answer her phone when she was away from her desk.

2. *Buck-passers.* Buck-passers are co-workers who shift their

work onto other people's desks. They do this by defining their own responsibilities as narrowly as possible. They are adept at determining why certain tasks are someone else's responsibility.

Shirley reported the following problem: "The lady on the switchboard seems to transfer calls to me when she isn't sure whom the caller should be talking to. I'm too busy with my own work to do part of her work too!"

Shirley should first check her job description to see if that task is part of her assigned duties. If not, she should talk to her boss. She would start the conversation, "I have a problem and I need your help in solving it. Sally, on switchboard, is transferring calls to me when she isn't sure who the caller should be talking to. Am I supposed to do this, or should I suggest she put the calls through to someone else?" This will allow her boss to know what's going on, and to decide what he or she wants Shirley to do about the problem.

Other buck-passers refuse to admit they have made a mistake. They say, "Who me? I didn't do that!" when they know they're at fault.

Deal with this by obtaining as much factual information as you can to prove that the person did do what they did. Again, talk to your supervisor about your concerns over co-workers' failure to take responsibility for their mistakes. Explain that you know anyone can make a mistake, but that it hurts you and other staff if co-workers try to pretend their errors are someone else's fault.

3. *Putter-offers.*   Here are five major types of putter-offers:

   1. *Hurry-up Type.*   They wait until the last minute and work around the clock to meet deadlines.
   2. *I'll Decide Tomorrow.*   They postpone decisions until events resolve the situation or a decision is forced on them.
   3. *Perfectionists.*   They must complete all tasks faultlessly, no matter how insignificant. (These people need to learn to discriminate between important and unimportant assignments.)
   4. *I'll Show 'Em.*   They delay completing assignments as a way of retaining a sense of personal power and control. This normally

happens when they're delegated a task they don't want to do, or feel someone else should do.

5. *Muddler.* They put off work because of bad habits, poor organization or lack of set procedures. They may go in circles, getting less and less accomplished as time goes on. These are the kind of people who start something, but leave it for another task before completing the original one.

Sandy found that at every month end she had to keep after her co-worker Joe to submit information she needed to complete her own report. She'd start reminding Joe a week ahead, then the day ahead. Finally, she went in at the last minute and insisted that he give her the report.

She could try the feedback technique and, if that didn't work, she could submit her report without Joe's information. If it was required information, she should put, "Information not available from ... [Joe's] department." That way, Joe would take the flack, not Sandy.

Another solution would be for Sandy to ask her boss to alleviate the problem. In this case her supervisor would normally talk to Joe's boss to straighten up the difficulty.

AGGRESSIVE BEHAVIOUR

The suggestions in earlier chapters on dealing with aggressive behaviour will be useful for resolving problems with this type of co-worker. An assertive response is usually the best course of action.

1. *Over-achievers and competitive types.* If some of your co-workers are over-achievers who try to make you feel inadequate, do the best you can. Don't let a co-worker try to set standards for you. Performance standards with your company should be based on average performance, not high or over-achievers' performance. Speak to your supervisor if you feel the standards of performance are unfair.

Jill had trouble with a co-worker, Sue, who was forever competing with her, even in the most trivial things. For instance, Sue kept challenging Jill to take a typing test with her to see who could type faster. Jill had done this on her noon hour twice already, and found she typed 65 w.p.m. with two errors. Sue typed 80 w.p.m. with eight errors, and felt she was a better typist. In reality, Sue spent much of her time at work correcting her errors. Jill objected when Sue called her a poor sport because she refused to do a third test.

Jill used the feedback technique to let Sue know how she felt about Sue's competitive approach to things. "Sue, it's not important to me who's the better typist, but I am getting upset because you keep insisting I compete with you. Why do you feel you always have to be the best in everything you do?"

"I like to win."

"Have you ever considered what others might be feeling when you try to force them to compete?"

"Everybody competes."

"Have you checked this out with others?"

"No, I haven't."

"Then maybe you should. I, for one, don't want to compete with others. As long as I'm doing the best job I can, I don't have to know I'm better than others."

Sue didn't concede completely, but thought more about her competitive approach to life. She saved competing for situations that warranted its use. Because she worked in the sales department of her firm, she was able to channel her competitiveness against other companies instead of against her co-workers.

2. *Critical types.*   When others (especially those whom you don't give a hoot about) criticize you unfairly, try the following:

Calmly acknowledge to your critic, that there *may* be some truth in what he or she says. This allows you to receive criticism comfortably, without becoming anxious or defensive, and gives no reward to those using the manipulative criticism. For example:

- *Agree with some aspect of the comment that is true.*
  "You're wearing that awful blouse today."
  "That's right, I am wearing this blouse."
- *Agree that the comment may possibly have some validity.*

"You're not very careful."

"Maybe I'm not very careful."

- *Agree with the logic of the comment.*

"If we bought a new truck now instead of keeping the old clunker, we'd be a lot safer on the road and wouldn't have these high repair bills."

"You're right. A new truck would have those advantages." (Rather than, "There you go, another way to spend our money.")

- *Allow for improvement.*

"Your dresses don't fit you correctly."

"I'm sure they could fit better."

- *Show empathy.*

"You're being very unfair."

"I can see that you feel that I'm unfair."

3. *Interrupters.*   Not all interruptions or interrupters are unjustified. A certain number of interruptions are part of any job, and no one expects co-workers to refrain altogether from social exchanges. It's when interruptions get out of hand that action is needed.

First, keep a log to determine who causes your interruptions, when, and for how long. You may find that a large portion of your day is spent dealing with interruptions. If you feel that they are keeping you from doing your "real" work, you may need to change your attitude. Perhaps dealing with these so-called interruptions is really an important part of your job, as important as completing reports. If that's the case, you need to respond by telling yourself, "That's my job calling."

If, however, your log reveals that many interruptions are not job-related, you need to analyse your findings more closely. Some of these interruptions may be your fault, in the sense that you may appear willing to be interrupted or may be reluctant to tell people you're too busy to talk to them. In this case you need to change your own behaviour.

Try doing the following:

- If people just want to chat, suggest they catch you at coffee break.

- Set time limits for meetings, and stick to them.
- Whenever possible meet people in their offices, so you can leave when you want to.

One of Debbie's co-workers used to ignore the fact that Debbie was on the phone and start talking to her. Debbie found it impossible to concentrate properly on her caller because of her co-worker's distracting behaviour.

Debbie could have handed her co-worker a piece of paper and a pen, indicating that she could leave a written message. Later, using feedback, Debbie could explain to her co-worker the difficulties caused by her behaviour.

PERSONALITY CONFLICTS

Sometimes the chemistry between you and a co-worker is just wrong. Normally you would just avoid such a person, but personality conflicts can be serious if your jobs require you to work together.

"I don't get along with my co-worker, and my boss won't do anything about the situation. We're at each other's throats all the time."

The first thing you could do is try to get the other employee to talk to you about the problem. You could start by saying, "Jim, we're always at each other's throats. This is affecting our productivity and both our chances for advancement in this company. Can you think of anything we can do to stop the problems we're having?"

If the initial attempt fails, you should then approach your supervisor directly. Start by saying, "I have a problem and I need your help in solving it. Jim and I seem to be on different wavelengths, and we're always at each other's throats. I've tried to resolve our differences, but it doesn't seem to have worked. Can you suggest anything I can do to help us get along better and be more productive?" If the conflict really is affecting your and Jim's productivity, your supervisor needs to be aware of it. It then becomes the supervisor's responsibility to resolve the problem.

CONDUCTING EFFECTIVE MEETINGS

Methods for chairing meetings differ slightly from those for dealing generally with co-workers, because the position of chair gives you some authority over the other participants. However, although the chair has certain powers that other members of the group do not, it is widely agreed that the most successful chairs do not "boss" the meeting. Their job is (a) to make it possible for all participants to contribute their expertise, and (b) to ensure that the purpose of the meeting is accomplished within the allotted time.

If you've ever headed a meeting, you know just how difficult it is to do both these things simultaneously. You want to move things along without missing a valuable contribution. You want to encourage contributions while controlling people who threaten to "take over" the meeting.

There are a variety of techniques that are helpful for dealing with the special problems of meetings. For instance, if someone's too talkative, you can interrupt with, "That's an interesting point. What do the rest of you think about this?" or, "We've been making George do all the work. What do the rest of you think about this?"

If the meeting's in progress and tempers flare, it's the chair's job to emphasize points of agreement and minimize points of disagreement. You can draw attention to the objectives of the meeting or ask direct questions relating to the topic. Or you could invite a contribution from a participant whom you know to be good at resolving disputes: "What do you think, Bill?"

If you suspect, even before a meeting starts, that there will be personality conflicts, talk to those involved before going to the meeting. Ask them to leave their negative attitudes towards each other out of the meeting room.

For instance, let's say you're a team leader for a project where several of your co-workers have to work together in harmony to get the job done. You know that Bill and Jim dislike each other because they had a heated argument at the last meeting and one of them stormed out. Before the next meeting you might say, "Bill, I've decided to talk to you before the meeting. I'm going to talk to Jim as well. I expect the two of you to participate fully at this meeting and you won't be able to do so if you get upset with each other. Can I count on you to co-operate?"

If you see any reluctance or resistance, you may have to add: "If we have a repeat performance of last week's meeting, I'll have to speak to your manager so we can get this project completed."

Here are some tips to enable you to handle the range of difficult participants you could encounter at a meeting:

Dealing with Problem Participants at Meetings

ACTION	POSSIBLE REASONS	WHAT TO DO
Participant is: Overly talkative — to the extent that other participants do not have an opportunity to contribute	Participant may be: — an "eager beaver"; — exceptionally well informed; — naturally wordy; — nervous.	— Interrupt with "That's an interesting point. . . . Let's see what everyone else thinks." — Directly call on others. — Suggest "Let's put others to work." — When the person stops for a breath, thank him or her, restate pertinent points and move on.
Argumentative — to the extent that others' ideas or opinions are rejected or others are treated unfairly.	— seriously upset about the issue under discussion; — upset by personal or job problems; — intolerant of others; — lacking in empathy; — a negative thinker.	— Keep your temper in check. — Try to find some merit in what's said; get group to see it too, then move on to something else. — Talk to the person privately and point out what his or her actions are doing to the rest of the group. — Try to gain the person's co-operation. — Encourage the person to concentrate on positives, not negatives.

Engaging in side conversations with others in the group.	— talking about something related to the discussion; — discussing a personal matter; — uninterested in the topic under discussion.	— Direct a question to the person. — Restate the last idea or suggestion expressed by the group, and ask for the person's opinion.
Unable to express self so that everyone understands.	— nervous, shy, excited; — not used to participating in discussions.	— Rephrase, restating what the person said, asking for confirmation of accuracy. — Allow person ample time to express self. — Help person along without being condescending.
Always seeking approval.	— looking for advice; — trying to get leader to support his or her point of view; — trying to put leader on the spot.	— Avoid taking sides, especially if the group will be unduly influenced by your point of view.
Bickering with another participant.	— carrying on an old grudge; — feeling very strongly about the issue.	— Emphasize points of agreement, minimize points of disagreement. — Direct participants' attention to the objectives of the meeting. — Mention time limits of the meeting. — Ask participants to shelve the issue for the moment.
Too quiet, unwilling to contribute.	— bored, indifferent, timid, insecure; — more knowledgeable or experienced than rest of the group.	— Direct questions to the person that you're fairly sure he or she can respond to. — Capitalize on the person's knowledge or experience by using them as a resource person.

Seeking attention.	— feeling inferior; — hiding a lack of knowledge by clowning around.	— Keep reminding the person about the topic being discussed. — Talk to the person privately. Point out what his or her actions are doing to the rest of the group.
Uninvolved and unwilling to commit to new tasks.	— lazy; — too busy already; — feeling he or she should not have been asked to the meeting in the first place.	— Ask for facts concerning the person's schedule. — Ask the person to volunteer for tasks (others in group must as well). — Make sure you ask the right people to future meetings.
Already too over-committed to other things to take on new tasks.	— unaware of own skills and abilities; — lacking in organizational skills.	— Ask for facts concerning the person's schedule. — Ask the person whether he or she is already overcommitted. — Tell the person you're counting on him or her. — Send the person to a time-management seminar.
A buck-passer who blames others for anything negative that happens and doesn't accept new tasks readily.	— unable to admit to making mistakes; — afraid to take risks.	— Make the person account for his or her actions. Ask for facts to back up allegations. — Privately ask why the person won't accept new tasks.

Suppose that you chair a meeting and delegate project assignments to a group. What do you do when you have a follow-up meeting and get these lame excuses?

a. "I didn't know I was responsible for that!"

b. "I didn't agree to do that!"

c. "I thought you didn't need that till next week."

These follow-through techniques may help you ensure that participants follow through too.

1. Set an agenda with time limits (give it to them before the meeting). Then follow the agenda.
2. During the meeting, delegate responsibility as required.
3. Set firm time deadlines for each commitment.
4. At the end of the meeting, ask each individual to confirm that he or she understands the task. "What is it you have to do before our meeting on December tenth? Bill . . . ? Sam . . . ? Sally . . . ?"
5. Follow up with written information (meeting notes).

CHAPTER SEVEN

DEALING WITH DIFFICULT SUBORDINATES

UNDERSTANDING THE SUPERVISORY ROLE

There are five essential elements to a supervisor's role. A person with full supervisory status has the responsibility for:

— delegating work
— checking work
— conducting performance appraisals
— disciplining subordinates
— hiring his or her own staff

1. *Delegating work.* This involves giving tasks to your subordinates for completion.

2. *Checking work.* This is done to see that employees complete tasks properly. You'll check the quantity and quality of the work performed and how long it took to complete.

3. *Conducting performance appraisals.* You and nobody else should have the responsibility for doing performance appraisals for all your subordinates. Your manager shouldn't do them, because he or she is not directly responsible for the work of your subordinates. Your manager might review your findings to see if they're fair, but you complete the appraisal on each employee you supervise.

4. *Disciplining subordinates.* Because your staff ends up making you look either good or bad, you need this control to correct

production and/or behaviour problems. However, because of the potential dangers of "wrongful dismissal" suits, many companies arrange for the actual firing of employees to be handled by those specially trained in its implementation.

5. *Hiring staff.* Whenever possible, have as much input as you can into the hiring of people who work for you. If you're on different wavelengths, it can be very difficult for you and your staff to work as a team.

Unfortunately, most employment interviewers decide whether they will hire a person within the first four minutes of the interview. They base their decision on what they see, hear and believe. They're evaluating the person's non-verbal language — how they walk, talk, sit and shake hands — and their verbal communication skills — how well they express themselves, their self-esteem level, etc.

At this point in the interview, the interviewers haven't even begun to ask the questions that should be the determiners of whether they hire the person or not.

If you have the responsibility of hiring staff, keep an open mind until the end of the interview. This way, your decision is based on more concrete information.

How does your supervisory position measure up? If you have only the first two responsibilities, you're in a "lead hand" position. This is a no-win situation for you. If you don't have the responsibility to conduct performance appraisals and discipline staff, you'll receive only token respect from your subordinates and will have little control over the outcome of their work.

If you don't have that control over your employees, and they do an unsatisfactory job — who looks bad? You do! If your company puts you in this position, talk to your manager and ask that you have the first four responsibilities (and the fifth, if at all possible). If your request is refused, ask that the manager look after the delegation and checking of responsibilities as well, and explain your reasons.

MOTIVATING EMPLOYEES
Of course, much more is involved in supervision than simply

assigning and checking work, assessing performance and disciplin-ing employees. Supervising people is an art that depends to a great extent on how well you can motivate people.

Supervisors must watch for the "Pygmalion effect" when trying to motivate staff. If a supervisor believes employees are smart, he or she will treat them that way. If a supervisor believes employees are capable of independent thought, he or she will treat them that way. Unfortunately if the supervisor believes that they are lazy, dumb or slow to pick up new ideas (or have any other undesirable attribute), he or she often treats them that way too. People respond to what they perceive is wanted from them. If supervisors expect high achievement, that's likely what they'll get. If supervisors expect low productivity, that's likely what they'll get.

Do you need to change your attitude towards the abilities of your staff? Are you letting the Pygmalion effect influence how you supervise your staff?

Some people are motivated by their interest in the work itself. Other motivators are the desire or need for:

— money
— acceptance by peers
— competition/challenge
— awards
— status
— better working conditions
— job security
— promotional opportunities
— a better office
— extra benefits
— recognition for good work

It's possible that your employees only hear from you when they've made mistakes. It's normal for all of us to want to receive praise and recognition for work well done. It's the best motivator of all. Give it a try. See if things change.

Be aware that it's not possible to motivate everyone — you just *can't* motivate some people. With unsatisfactory workers, start by spelling out exactly what you expect of them (document your requests properly). Then give them ample opportunity to improve their performance. If they refuse to conform, replace them with good workers. There are too many excellent people who are unemployed for companies to keep foot-draggers on the payroll. They just demotivate everyone around them.

Acquaint yourself with some of the standard procedures for managing human resources and try to get your company to use them, if it is not already doing so. Such basic tools of personnel management as job descriptions and performance appraisals help employees feel that they know what is expected of them and that their efforts are recognized. They can be confident that procedures are in place to allow them to develop their skills and earn promotions. The advantages of some of these management tools are discussed in the examples that follow.

1. Standard motivational management tools.
"My staff expect to receive credit for their contribution to my reports and projects."

As mentioned in the chapter on dealing with supervisors, the boss's failure to give them credit is a pet peeve of subordinates. It certainly can't hurt you if you give your staff credit for doing part of a report or project, can it? If you don't, you'll probably have demotivated them for the next report or project they're part of. The main goal of supervisors is to motivate staff to do their best work. Doesn't it make sense to give them credit for good work?

"My staff expects me to change their job descriptions to suit their own talents and abilities!"

Many progressive-thinking firms are doing just that. Instead of pushing employees to fit the needs of the company, many are adapting positions to match the employees' talents and abilities. Until all firms do this, employees must conform to the needs of the position they're hired to fill.

"I don't fully believe in job descriptions because they just encourage staff to state, 'That's not in my job description!' "

As discussed earlier, accurate, up-to-date job descriptions are essential for an employee to do good work. How can your staff possibly do a good job for you and your company if they don't know what's expected from them? Clearly define each task, giving standards of performance (quality, quantity and time) for each one. Then, and only then, will both you and your staff know what's expected of them.

"My training budget is nil, but my staff want and expect training."

It's not a nice place for a supervisor to be, but it happens in bad economic times. It's not always possible for companies to provide all the funds for training, but there can usually be some compromises. Some companies have employees sign a document stating that employees will have to reimburse their company for the cost of training, should they leave the company within two years of training. Alternatively, the company could pay for half the training costs.

If employees require training, the supervisor must show management the cost-effectiveness of the training. Itemize the ways in which the training will benefit the company. In particular, try to identify the financial benefits to the company. If the company still proves ungenerous, encourage staff to get the training themselves. Explain the benefits to them of additional future salary as compared to the cost of training—that it's an investment in their future.

"My staff want regular performance appraisals, but my company doesn't give them."

It's a standard practice in most businesses to have at least a yearly performance appraisal for each employee. As well, appraisals are often conducted at the end of the employee's probationary period. They're highly recommended, to make employees aware of how they're doing. Some firms offer performance appraisals after each special project.

There are many kinds of performance appraisals. Most are extremely poor because they evaluate subjective things such as attitude, judgment and initiative. This type of evaluation depends heavily on the mood of the person preparing the appraisal.

Instead, employees should be evaluated on whether they reached planned objectives. Each objective would include standards of performance. This method takes the uncertainty out of performance appraisals. Both the employee and the supervisor know exactly how the employee is doing because the evaluation is based on facts rather than on the supervisor's personal impressions.

If your company doesn't have regular performance appraisals, suggest it start to do so. State that you intend to have such appraisals for your own staff, even if the company doesn't. In many cases, when one department initiated an appraisal system, employees in other departments soon saw the benefits and lobbied for the system to be used company-wide. Try it — you've got nothing to lose.

"My company doesn't have a personnel department. How do I choose proper salary ranges for my staff?"

Call your competitors and find out what they pay people with skills and abilities like those of your staff. Watch newspaper advertisements describing positions like those in your company. Don't be cheap — it's better to overpay slightly than to underpay and lose good employees.

"Should I follow the trend of replacing older, more expensive staff with younger, less expensive staff?"

This is a tough question to answer. It's often the only answer some companies see to economic problems. A senior, long-term employee who may be five years away from retirement and earns £25,000 could be replaced by a more junior person at £15,000 a year.

Many companies have been offering their senior staff early retirement, as a humane compromise. Some firms, however, simply decide to let their senior, more expensive staff go. Not only is this usually devastating for the employee, but other staff soon begin to wonder when their turn will come. Employees the company may wish to keep may seek other jobs and leave at inconvenient times. Morale may suffer and affect productivity adversely.

Though there aren't any easy answers to this problem, companies need to consider the pros and cons very carefully before deciding to follow this trend.

2. Motivating aggressive employees.

A real test of a supervisor's skill are employees who appear to be poorly motivated but have the potential to be great assets to the company. Such employees often have a great deal of energy that shows itself in negative, aggressive, even trouble-making behaviour. This negative behaviour could be caused by:

— the feeling that they lack job security;
— the feeling that they lack the necessary education, experience or knowledge;
— lack of self-esteem or pride in their own skills, abilities and achievements;
— work that underuses their skills and abilities;
— the feeling of not fitting in with their work group (perhaps because of racial and/or cultural differences).

Those who believe they don't fit into their positions for whatever reason may act aggressively towards their company, top man-age-ment, supervisors, co-workers or clients. Supervisors seeking to "turn around" employees of this type could:

— give authentic compliments on the work completed;
— explain to the employees how valuable their efforts are to their fellow workers (part of the team);
— explain the importance of their jobs to the company;
— show that their training and other qualifications equip them to do more than just a satisfactory job;
— provide some measure of recognition for their work accom-plishments;
— bring them into group situations: ask for their advice;
— carefully describe the responsibilities of their position and set *reachable* performance standards.

Many aggressive employees have a great deal to offer. They may be very success-oriented and willing to accept challenges and to set high standards for themselves in order to achieve recognition. Their energy level is often high, so that supervisors may find it difficult to keep them constructively occupied. Power also stimulates these people, and they may respond well if given some authority as soon as they're able to handle it. Delegate responsibilities that allow them to take charge, but watch carefully for abuse of other co-workers or clients. These employees may be poor delegators and unwilling to ask for the help that they need. They may prefer to work alone. Give them that chance if possible. Such employees also tend to enjoy variety, so try to change their tasks often.

3. Motivating employees who are reluctant to change.

When supervisors want to make changes in the methods their subordinates use to complete assignments, they're often surprised by the resistance they meet. This is especially true right now with so many technological changes happening.

Do you have trouble adjusting to change? Can you think of a situation that's facing you now that involves change? If you're able to identify one, ask yourself, "What can go wrong if I refuse to change?" Then decide what the advantages will be of changing now, rather than later, when you have no choice.

Supervisors and trainers need to be aware of the stages people go through when adjusting to change in order to help them make the transition as smoothly as possible. There are three phases in the process:

1. *Unfreezing.* During this initial stage you require employees to give up their regular way of doing things and identify new methods. This involves breaking old habits.
2. *Changing.* The new pattern of behaviour or new way of doing something is explained and taught. Before this can be done the supervisor needs to identify the advantages of the change and the reasons why it might provoke resistance. Ways of overcoming objections to the change should also be identified.
3. *Refreezing.* Employees use of the new method is monitored until it takes hold. Supervisors must catch die-hards who are determined to do it the old way. This can take up to three months of constant surveillance.

Overcoming objections to change

New systems, methods and designs won't work unless you get people to accept new ideas. You might have to sell your ideas. This is where planning comes in. For example, suppose you've found a faster way of processing clients' orders. Before explaining the new system to others, prepare by:

a. writing a summary of the existing method;
b. determining the advantages and disadvantages of this method;
c. writing a summary of the new method;
d. determining the advantages and disadvantages of the new method;
e. anticipating the objections others will raise and deciding what you will say to defend your new idea.

The following checklist will help you cope with objections from others more effectively.

- Anticipate and prepare for as many possible objections as you can. Develop a plan for handling each of them.
- Ask staff to explain their objections in very specific terms with examples.
- Don't be content with superficial reasons for resistance to a change. Dig until you discover the real reasons.
- Work out a practical way of overcoming each objection if you possibly can.
- If you're unable to overcome an objection, try to find a way to compensate for it.
- Rally enough benefits to win the person's support and co-operation despite the objection.
- Find a way to ease the person's mind, to make it less risky to go along with you despite the objection.
- With habitual or chronic objectors, introduce your idea gradually. Don't try to get immediate acceptance or compliance. The objection may be nothing more than a delaying tactic — the person's natural resistance to change.
- Consider bringing up significant objections yourself instead of

waiting for others to do so. Then explain how these can be overcome.

CORRECTING OR DISCIPLINING EMPLOYEES

Sometimes supervisors have to correct their employees' behaviour. Whether the outcome is positive or negative depends on how they do this. There are two basic kinds of criticism, constructive and destructive.

1. *Constructive Criticism.*   Constructive criticism attempts to correct the behaviour of the person. The person offering the criticism explains how he or she feels about the behaviour that needs to be changed and gives the other person a chance to correct the behaviour. For example, "Joan, I'm finding that your gum-cracking is distracting me from doing my work. Would you like this roll of peppermints instead?"

2. *Destructive Criticism.* Destructive criticism focuses on the person rather than the behaviour. For example, "Joan, stop cracking your gum! You're the most selfish person I know! You don't care anything about the people who have to work with you!"

   Joan probably feels the need to defend herself (she has been personally attacked). She'll probably retaliate, and her negative behaviour will likely continue.

The following communication skills are useful when it's necessary to discipline or criticize a subordinate.

Supportive questions

These are responses that show acceptance and understanding of the feelings of the person you're talking with, and acknowledge his or her efforts to grow and change.

1. "Do you feel you're not getting co-operation from . . . ?
2. "How can I help you get this roadblock removed?"
3. "You believe you have the skills to complete this task?"

Exploratory questions
These are responses made to encourage further examination even though the facts may be unpleasant.

1. "Tell me more about that."
2. "What seems to be the difficulty here?"
3. "When did this first start?"
4. "How does this relate to your performance?"

"I never know how to start an interview where I have to correct someone's behaviour. Should I start by telling the person all their good qualities and attributes, before I concentrate on the ones I want changed?"

Start by giving a brief overall summary of the employee's behaviour (trying to emphasize the good-news aspect), then discuss the behaviour you want to correct, and end by refocusing on the employee's strengths.

Think back to conversations you've had with former bosses. Did you hear one word they said while they were expressing their views on what you did right? Probably not. We seem to wait for that special word "but," and we seldom hear anything that precedes it. Most people do things right about 95 per cent of the time, but feel hurt about the 5 per cent that requires correction.

Because of this, you should start by talking about the 5 per cent they have done wrong. Explain that the important thing is that they learn from their mistakes and don't make them again. Then you can use the rest of the interview to tell them what they've done right. This concludes the meeting with positive feelings and results in a more pleasant ending for both of you. The employee knows what has to be corrected, but isn't left with a feeling of failure.

DELEGATING
Many supervisors fail because they lack the ability to delegate tasks properly to their staff. They make excuses such as:

- "I need this completed right now. I could finish this job and three others if I did it myself. It would take twice as long to train someone else, then check to see they did it right!"

- "This job is so important that only I can do it."
- "I'm afraid my staff will fail."
- "I can do this better than anyone else."
- "I don't want my people to think I'm a tyrant."

Many hidden reasons are behind the above explanations. Supervisors don't delegate enough tasks because:

- They fear a loss of control. It reflects directly on them if their staff make mistakes.
- They fear losing their jobs. Some supervisors feel that if they delegate too much, they'll have no job left to do. Another expression is, "Suppose someone on my staff becomes better than me?"

Many supervisors are unaware of an important factor in delegation. Failure to groom staff to succeed them may result in their being overlooked themselves when a more responsible position is being filled. Proving there is someone ready to take over their existing position is one way of showing they are eligible for promotion. (One way to prove this is to ensure there is at least one employee who can be placed in an acting position when the supervisor is away.)

DEALING WITH PREJUDICE AGAINST WOMEN SUPERVISORS

Anti-female prejudice is found in both men and women who believe that men are superior to women and that the world should be male-dominated. This is one of the most serious problems women still face in the work place. How should women respond to such prejudice?

Some anti-female attitudes are openly expressed, so that you're in no doubt that a particular person is out to keep women in their "place." However, many people aren't aware that their attitudes could be considered biased. These are often older men, or men whose upbringing or home situation kept women in traditionally subservient positions. Many of these men call women "dear" because women are dear to them. Such men protect women; they feel it's their duty to do so. This type of man doesn't mean to harm women and usually doesn't understand why women are offended by certain remarks. In these cases a gentle response is necessary. Use of the feedback technique will give these men the opportunity to change their behaviour.

Many older women also suffer from an anti-female bias. They have been conditioned to believe women should be subservient and think of women who compete with others, supervise men or hold positions of power as unfeminine. They look down on such women, especially if they aren't married or have no intention of having children.

Anti-female attitudes are not uncommon in younger and middle-aged women. For instance, women who won't accept orders from female supervisors unconsciously feel that only men should be supervisors. They question the ability of their female supervisors and make things difficult for them.

Support staff (who are still mainly women) normally go out of their way to keep their supervisors (who are still usually male) organized, on time and comfortable. They nurture their supervisors (bring them coffee, remind them of appointments, open their mail). When a woman is appointed to a supervisory position, the nurturing may stop, unless she's on top of things. She sometimes has to let her staff know that she expects the same kind of help that the former male supervisor received.

1. Older subordinates.

Janet had a problem that at one time was rare but is quite common now. By the time she was twenty-five, she held the position of clerical supervisor. Her college education had prepared her for the position and she had four years' experience in an office. However, she found herself unprepared to supervise women almost twice her age. These women had an average of ten to fifteen years' office experience. They were openly hostile to her and quite unco-operative.

Janet decided to ask Sarah, one of the less-hostile older women, into her office to discuss the problem. Sarah was honest. She admitted she had been surprised and disappointed when Janet had been "hired off the street" as her supervisor. She had pictured someone her own age or older filling the position — possibly one of her peer group or someone whose experience she felt would give her the "right" to supervise. Instead, she found a woman the same age as her daughter in the role.

She admitted that when Janet complimented her on a job well done she felt patronized, and when she was disciplined she felt defensive. Once these feelings were brought out into the open, the two women were able to start over. Janet now understood the reasons for Sarah's antagonism and could deal with it better. Sarah had clarified why she felt as she did and made an effort to change her attitude towards Janet.

Soon Janet called a meeting with the rest of her staff to discuss the situation with them. She said that she understood how they felt and explained to them what she expected from them. She then added that she was relying on them to co-operate and asked each staff member, "Can I count on you in the future?" One employee, Julie, appeared reluctant to make such a commitment, so Janet knew she would have to keep an eye on her. Soon the woman's low productivity and negative attitude made it necessary for Janet to discipline her. She again explained to Julie what she expected from her and what the consequences would be if Julie kept on producing sloppy work. Unfortunately, Julie never did accept Janet. She kept on producing sloppy work and eventually had to be fired.

Janet fared better with the others. When she noticed a decided change in attitude and productivity, she thanked them for their understanding and co-operation.

Traditionally, society has taught us that the older woman (the mother or the aunt) knows more so therefore should be treated with respect. Switching roles is disconcerting to both the young female supervisor (who's artificially in the position of the mother) and the older female employee (who's now in the position of the daughter seeking approval). These feelings revolve around power, and who should rightly have it. Thre is no cut-and-dried solution to the problem.

2. Male subordinates.
Barbara supervised a staff of three men. She was an engineer and the men were technologists. Her subordinates didn't seem to listen to

her and insisted on doing things their way. Fortunately, before taking the position, she had made sure that she had received proper supervisory training. This boosted her self-confidence.

Barbara found it necessary to conduct a disciplinary interview when one of her male subordinates refused to do a task assigned to him. This was a case of insubordination (a very serious infraction) that could have led to the dismissal of the employee. She handled it herself, and placed a strong written warning on the employee's file, stating that he would be fired if his negative behaviour continued. She made sure her supervisor was aware of her actions, and he commended her on the competent way she had handled the touchy situation.

3. Labelling by subordinates.
Margaret, a supervisor, had been labelled "aggressive" by her subordinates and co-workers. She felt that she was just doing her job the way she had seen other supervisors do it.

She had copied her male counterparts' behaviour and language. It didn't work in her case and she had been labelled an "aggressive female."

Her appearance and body language suggested that she was a forceful, self-assured, rather pushy individual. These qualities are readily accepted in men but less readily in women. I explained that her tone of voice could be the problem, or possibly her forceful body language.

Questioning revealed that she tended to give instructions in the form of orders rather than requests — "You will . . . " rather than, "I would like you to. . . ." She agreed to tone down her speech and body language. It worked.

DEALING WITH UNPRODUCTIVE BEHAVIOUR
The term "unproductive behaviour" covers a multitude of items, from intractable inefficiency to theft. To correct some of these you need little more than well-honed communication skills. Others may require you to exercise all the supervisory and managerial skills at your command.

1. Buck-passing employees.

In today's complex managerial environment, it's becoming increasingly important to avoid even minor errors. Buck-passing can be a symptom of a supervisor's failure to delegate responsibility correctly or to define responsibilities clearly. Formal policy-and-procedures manuals that define responsibility would eliminate some of this buck-passing.

It's not enough for supervisors to tell employees how to do their jobs. They must also explain exactly what their responsibilities are. For example, "Wilma, you're responsible for correctly matching freight bills to the duplicate of the receiving report."

"What if there are differences?"

"It's part of your duty to note the differences on the voucher to Accounts Payable. Any mistakes in matching will be your fault. Any questions?"

Even a well-qualified employee like Wilma will make mistakes. However, she'll make fewer and fewer mistakes and won't attempt to pass the buck if you keep reminding her of her responsibilities.

Try not to overdiscipline for any errors. Too heavy a disciplinary hand only invites excuses (e.g., "The dispatcher said it's okay to approve trucking bills, so I thought this was okay too." Or, "Don't blame me for that one! John said it was okay to approve it.").

Overly severe disciplinary action for mistakes has other adverse effects besides buck-passing. It causes lying, cheating and hiding of mistakes. The concealment of mistakes causes irreparable harm to the company. Service failures can be expensive. The cost of the immediate replacement of the service plus the lowered image of the company results in decreases in sales or service volume.

From time to time, supervisors should set an example by admitting to mistakes themselves in the presence of their subordinates. This can demonstrate to others that passing the buck is not acceptable.

2. Bottleneck employees.

"The work isn't getting out because John's sitting on it!" Bottlenecks are a frequent management complaint. A bottleneck is someone or something that stops the flow of work. It often results in employees' inactivity while they wait for the bottleneck to clear. The causes could be attributable to either the design of the work flow or the employee's personal work habits. If you suspect poor design of the work flow, try this simple test. Have another employee assume the duties of the employee in the problem area. If there's still a bottleneck (after a period of training), make changes in the work-flow arrangement.

Bottleneck employees typically have the following characteristics:

— tendency to be derailed by relatively minor problems;
— not enough training;
— low decision-making capability;
— ignorance of productivity requirements;
— lack of team-member identity;
— job insecurity;
— unusual fear of making mistakes;
— incompatibility with co-workers leading to lack of co-operation.

If there's no indication that the bottleneck is deliberately caused, perhaps the bottleneck employee is not clear about what you want. The supervisor should reinforce the employee's training. During this retraining, the supervisor can see if the employee is comprehending the job in detail, demonstrate to the employee how to perform the various tasks and then guide the employee under direct observation. The emphasis should be on techniques that can speed up completion of the job.

Employees should know how their job fits in with others in the company. They then have knowledge of the consequences of their own good or bad performance.

Most stick-in-the-mud employees don't really want to be that way. Most want to feel that they are co-operating in achieving common goals. The secret is to make everyone in the work force have a common goal. Supervisors should enlist the help of other employees by saying:

"Say, Tom, can you show Richard how we can move that project faster?"

"Richard, let Tom show you a couple of techniques for pushing the stuff through that we need now."

An important element in removing the bottleneck is to make the problem employee want to put the work out faster. The paying of a few compliments here and there improves confidence among slower employees. It permits them to have a greater feeling of job security and certainly reduces tensions. The bottleneck employee who feels more in control will have less fear of making mistakes. In short, some additional coaching, coupled with a reduction in tension, may free the employee to move faster.

3. Error-prone employees.

There are two basic kinds of accidents. One type results from systems design. The methods or techniques used permit a certain number of errors. Constant improvement of the system reduces the error rate. However, no matter how well the system is designed, the human factor must be considered as well. The following conditions may be at fault:

— inadequate job training;
— limited written instructions;
— too many subordinates reporting to one supervisor;
— too few intermediate levels of supervision;
— dull work environment;
— employees bored with their jobs;
— no studies done to determine error causes;
— high employee-turnover rate.

Auto-insurance companies recognize that some drivers are more prone to having accidents than the general population of drivers. Some employees are more likely to make mistakes than others. Deliberate mistakes should result in disciplinary actions, up to and including firing of the employee. However, most mistakes aren't intentional. They're caused by a variety of factors, including errors in judgment on the part of management or lack of employee training. Suggested steps to reduce errors are:

1. Determine the nature of errors.
2. Revise the system to improve error detection.

3. Use a senior employee as a coach to an error-prone employee.
4. Appeal to the employee's pride of workmanship.
5. Have a chat with an error-prone employee to review causes of mistakes.

Most employees like to feel that they're earning their pay. Part of that feeling of pride stems from their opinion that their work has few, if any, errors. Therefore, they appreciate help, when it is offered gracefully, in improving their own pride in their work. One method of attack, is to provide an employee-coach for the error-prone employee.

Senior employees who are proficient in their work can help isolate the *causes* of problem employees' errors. Rather than catching mistakes *after* the fact and taking corrective action, they can provide instruction to help avoid errors. The problem employee may simply need to be told which points require additional attention (e.g., "Bryan, can you spend a little more effort on re-checking?" or, "Marcia, can you pay a little more attention to these types of items?").

To reinforce pride of workmanship, don't let employees describe their positions as "just a janitor" or "just a receptionist." Be ready to explain their importance to the smooth running of your company.

4. Daydreamers.

We all daydream, but some people do it to excess — to a point where it results in low productivity, errors and accidents. Some jobs lend themselves more to employee daydreaming than others and need more thorough monitoring.

It's not always fair to pin the blame for daydreaming on employees. Their jobs may be so boring that they can't keep their minds on the task. Robotic-like duties invite employee daydreaming.

Work that requires employee creativity should have an environment that's conducive to creativity. Where different and varied types of work proceed through a section, it's advisable to use job rotation to alleviate monotony. Adding flexibility in the method of performing the job will allow the employees to decide how to handle individual steps. Such flexibility permits employees to think about how they want to handle particular jobs. This in turn increases alertness and reduces monotony. The use of job rotation provides some cross-training (more people know different jobs). This gives supervisors a greater flexibility in the use of their staff and provides more than one worker who is qualified to fill the position.

Jobs should be designed to hold the employee's attention. Tasks performed while the person is standing discourage daydreaming. Better design of the work area can also help. The decor of the work area is of some importance. Desks or work areas need not be the same colour. Make every effort to remove monotony in the work environment. Recommended steps are:

1. Evaluate the environment. Make any changes possible.
2. Revise work flow to reduce monotony.
3. Develop alternative methods and order of steps to accomplish the work.
4. Where possible, let the employee decide what he or she is to produce that day.
5. Identify employees who require constant supervisor prompting to improve attentiveness.

No matter what efforts you make to dispel daydreaming, some employees remain lost in the clouds. Only constant supervisory attention can dispel the problem and keep the employee on his or her toes. In this case, a discussion between the supervisor and the employee is definitely in order. It may become necessary to replace the worker.

5. Time-wasters.

a. Personal telephone calls

Nothing's as annoying to a supervisor as watching an employee receive an excessive number of personal telephone calls. It's not just that the lines are being tied up; the flow of work is also interrupted. If employees waste company time, they waste the company money allotted for their salaries. Employees should keep personal calls to a minimum. After all, they are at a place of business, and personal-life requirements should wait until after work.

Employees who conduct personal business on company time are often overlooked for promotions. Most don't even understand what they've done to hamper their progress in the company.

Strategies to alleviate this problem include:

1. Telling employees to limit personal phone calls to important or emergency calls, which should be kept short and sweet. Have them advise their friends and relatives about the company policy. No more than one or two personal calls a day should be necessary.

2. Requiring the switchboard operator to ask an incoming caller for his or her name and to say, "What company do you represent?" That question alone may be enough to reduce non-business calls and their duration. The switchboard operator might keep track of non-business calls for one or two days and submit a report to the supervisor of each section. Interviews with errant employees can then be arranged to reinforce the policy.

3. Making sure employees realize that their behaviour may be keeping them from being promoted to a higher position.

b. Coffee- and lunch-break abuses

Studies show that breaks in the work schedule increase production. At the same time, supervisors need to guard against the tendency of employees to slow down in anticipation of coffee or lunch breaks. Many employees will extend their breaks if there is no pressure on them not to do so. After the break, work should begin right away. If you've identified this as a problem, be visible immediately before and after breaks. This enables you to observe abuses directly and to encourage more productive use of your employees' time. After the break, you could hand out assignments or check employees' progress.

Only a conscientious effort on the part of supervisory personnel will segregate those who occasionally abuse breaks from those who consistently do so. Despite supervisory efforts, some employees will continue to abuse coffee and lunch breaks. This warrants formal disciplinary action (written warning on file, suspension for a day, etc.).

c. Absenteeism

Many employees will go to work even with a runny nose and a fever. They refuse to take advantage of their company's sick-pay policy. Many feel they don't wish to take sick leave for minor ailments because they may need the leave when they're really sick. Others feel that no one else can handle their job as well as they can. They feel responsible for their performance. To them, it's part of the ethic of being a good worker. The supervisor should recognize the sacrifices made by this kind of worker. When that type of employee is out ill, he or she is usually too sick to perform any kind of work at all. Such employees are assets to any company. Unfortunately, however, most companies also have their share of employees who abuse their sick-leave privileges. In fact, *in any normal working day, usually from 4 to 6 per cent of all employees are absent from work.*

Absenteeism disrupts the flow of work and causes delays and production problems. The quality of work suffers because employees replaced by others are not as well trained or because overtime is needed to complete the extra work.

Because the costs to the company of abuses of sick leave are high, all supervisors need to take steps to discourage unwarranted absenteeism. Such steps include:

— enforcing the rules. Otherwise employees will keep on abusing them, and others may be encouraged to do so as well;
— determining if there are absenteeism patterns. The five major types of unwarranted absenteeism are listed below along with some strategies for dealing with them. (NOTE: Some solutions may not be compatible with your company or union agreements. Make sure you're aware of these before acting.)

(i) Chronic absenteeism

Chronic absentees are often negative thinkers. Everyday frustrations and pressures easily overwhelm them. They consistently have unwarranted absences that usually follow a pattern. This type of employee calls and says, "Sorry, boss, but I can't make it in today."

You may be tempted to reply, "I'm sorry you're sick. Stay away until you're feeling better." However, don't say that. Don't worry, such employees will stay away until they feel a lot better, with or without your blessing. They view their sick leave as a right.

How many times a year do employees pull that line before you consider them chronic absentees? One company identifies problem employees by eight or more absences of one or more days each month in a year.

For those suspected of abusing their sick-leave privileges, the supervisor should call the employee at the end of each work day and say, "Orson, how are you coming along? I'm calling to see if you expect to be back to work tomorrow."

Using this tactic allows two beautiful spin-off benefits to happen. First, you've determined that the absent employee is really at home. Of course, he or she could have been at the doctor's, but not *every* time you called. Second, you will discourage the employee from taking sick leave for minor ailments or to accomplish personal chores.

When the employee returns to work, the supervisor should:

— state, "Sure missed you yesterday. We really need and depend on you."
— describe the problems the employee's absence caused the department.
— encourage the employee to be in more often.
— explain the consequences if similar instances occur too often.

Innocent absenteeism, even if it's excessive, doesn't warrant disciplinary action. On the other hand, an employee's inability to report regularly for work, *for whatever reasons*, provides grounds for termination of employment. In such cases:

1. The employer must be able to document the employee's absences. These absences must be well beyond what any reasonable person would consider acceptable. The employee must have deviated substantially and unduly from the average level of attendance of other employees.
2. The employer should ascertain the reasons for absence and

should give the employee a chance to state his or her case, and to be accompanied by a colleague whilst doing so.

3. The employer must be able to demonstrate that the excessive-absenteeism problem has been persistent. It must have continued despite *documented* attempts by the employer to have it corrected. The supervisor must keep a record of his or her efforts to counsel the employee and to determine the underlying reasons for absences. The supervisor must be able to show that he or she has been reasonable and compassionate and has taken exenuating circumstances into account.

4. Warnings should be issued and, where appropriate, time for improvement given. The employer should consider whether suitable alternative employment is available.

5. The employer must be able to present convincing reasons explaining why he or she feels there's little or no likelihood of improvement.

An employee who falsifies a doctor's certificate should receive a written warning, which is placed on his or her file, or possibly termination. The degree of discipline depends on the circumstances.

When an employee's excessive absenteeism is due to a drinking or drug problem, the employer should consider whether it is appropriate to treat the problem as a medical, rather than a disciplinary matter. The employee should be encouraged to seek medical help and treatment. However, if the employer can demonstrate that the employment relationship cannot continue, the employee may be discharged. The company *must* be able to prove that it has made an honest effort to help the employee to correct the illness.

(ii) Truant absenteeism

These absentees typically decide to enjoy themselves (go golfing, perhaps) rather than do what they consider dull, repetitious work that they believe wastes their abilities. They feel the need to escape the humdrum environment of work. This can lock them into a vicious circle, because these people are seldom considered for the promotions they think they need and deserve. To help them lose this need to escape, the supervisor should:

1. Confront them with their absenteeism record.
2. Ask why it's happening.
3. Encourage them to use their sick leave properly. Explain that SICK LEAVE IS A PRIVILEGE, NOT A RIGHT and should be used only for *their own* authentic illnesses, *not for personal reasons or their children's or spouse's illnesses.*
4. Make sure that they are aware that their absence record is a major factor keeping them from being promoted.
5. Identify rewards (e.g., a promotion) that may be obtained with good attendance. This is far better than using punishment (written warning on file) to bring about changes in behaviour.

(iii) Naive absenteeism

Many employees believe that management expects and condones phony absences. These employees also believe that if they have sick leave coming, they have the right to take it whenever they please. Employee morale breaks down when employees get away with calling in sick and get paid for the day, when they weren't sick at all. While it's difficult to determine with complete certainty who is truly ill and who isn't, supervisors should make sure that employees don't abuse sick leave. To deal with this, supervisors should:

1. Confront employees regarding their absenteeism record.
2. Explain what sick leave is all about (a privilege, not a right). Tell them that they're doing important work and that the company suffers when they're away.
3. Encourage employees to use absences properly — for legitimate illnesses.
4. Ask employees to identify what effects their absence has had on other employees.

(iv) Abusive absenteeism

Some employees will be away for any and every minor ailment. They demonstrate little sense of responsibility for any required productivity. It is of little concern to them if their absence means that other workers have to carry a larger work load or that their company will suffer economically. These employees are usually unhappy, feel victimized and believe that others receive favouritism. They break company rules and have many conflicts with their supervisors. They pick fights and believe that they're always right and others are always wrong. Should you have to deal with such employees:

1. Be direct about the penalties for continuing the abuse. "Your job's on the line unless you conform to the rules of this company." Tell them you'll have to replace them if their record doesn't improve, that they must produce doctor's reports for absenteeism, etc. Stick to the facts and be firm and clear about the consequences.
2. Compliment them on the work they do when they are conforming to the rules.

(v) Legitimate absenteeism
Authentic illnesses, bereavement, jury duty and necessary personal business, such as dentist and doctor's appointments, are legitimate reasons for taking time off. However, employers shouldn't pay sick leave to those who take time off for their children's illnesses (this should be time off without pay, unless company policy states otherwise).

Absenteeism Policies
When industries rely on individual performance, any absence is a disruption in the flow of service to customers. To help reduce absenteeism, many companies have implemented stiffer proof-of-illness procedures. They may:

— require a doctor's certificate for any absence of three or more sick days a week;
— require a doctor's certificate for *any* absence due to illness, or after a holiday weekend;
— require a complete physical examination by the company doctor if the employee is away more than ten days in any one year.

6. Poor housekeepers.

Many consider good housekeeping as window dressing. They explain, "I know where everything is on my desk!" It's when they're away because of illness that their messiness causes difficulties. Others who take over can't find things. In fact, poor housekeepers often *don't* know where everything is, and an unduly messy work area may be a sign of inefficiency. Excessive untidiness can result in:

- missing records or files;
- lost or misplaced tools or equipment;
- high supply costs;
- an improper mix of parts and inventory;
- contamination of the product;
- high scrap and reworking costs;
- a poor balance of finished products in inventory;
- high machine downtime;
- a poor safety record;
- low employee morale and reluctance to work overtime;
- discipline problems and labour turnover.

Motivate your employees to maintain a tidy work area by your example. Good housekeeping habits are more easily encouraged among your staff if your own office is kept neat and clean. Encourage clean-ups at the end of each day. If you spot employees whose work stations look messy heading for the door, stop them. Ask them to organize their work station before leaving. You may have to provide a written checklist of housekeeping activities they are to follow.

7. Dishonest employees.

There was a time when thefts from inventory affected only industries that had attractive types of inventory. Increasingly, however, all types of inventory are becoming subject to theft. Not only completed assemblies, but also parts and even raw materials are being stolen.

Employees who take home a few coloured pencils for their children may not cost the company much but they set a bad attitudinal example. Some employees go far beyond a few pencils. Theft is often a way of "getting back at management." Some of these people will steal far more than they could ever use. Usually, employees who constantly steal are unsatisfactory employees, not only because of their thieving, but for other reasons as well. It's not just that they have low regard for company property, but they think little of the company that employs them.

It's not economically justifiable to lock everything up, nor is it possible to catch all the culprits. However, if management removes some of the temptations, they'll have fewer losses. Having only one or two people in charge of the company office supplies is one way of cutting down on pilfering. Having employees sign for stationery and equipment is another.

SUPERVISING FORMER PEERS
How should you handle the first day on the job where you're suddenly responsible for supervising your former peers? You'll likely fail if you don't handle that first day or week properly. It's necessary to remove any feelings of envy and jealousy your new subordinates might have.

Your manager will usually call a meeting to introduce you to your new staff, then leave so you can take over the meeting.

If you anticipate hard feelings, deal with your former co-workers' feelings first. Start by saying, "I know a few of you applied for and wanted this promotion. I can understand that you may feel a little upset that I got the position instead of you. The company chose me, so what we do from now on depends on how all of us work together. I need your support to handle my job properly. In return, I'll do everything I can to be a good supervisor. Can I count on you for your support?"

Ask those present, one by one, to indicate to you whether you can rely on them: "Margie—how about you, can I count on your support?" "Dave?" Cover every employee in the room. If your staff have made a verbal commitment to you, they're much more likely to co-operate in the future.

If you detect reluctance to make the commitment, don't let it pass. In a private interview, say, "Margie, I detect some hesitancy in your reply. What can I do to make the situation a little easier for you?"

If she still balks, you'll have to keep your eye on her. She might try to sabotage your efforts. If she does, you'll have to be on top of the situation and implement immediate disciplinary action. Don't be afraid to do it. Nip the problem in the bud; don't let it grow and flourish and contaminate the others in your section.

DEALING WITH PERSONALITY CLASHES

When two of your staff have a personality clash, how and when should you intervene?

If two employees don't get along, the one who suffers most is their supervisor. You may find that Bob and George are excellent workers, but harass each other and fail to co-operate. If the conflict arises from a work-related cause and affects their productivity or that of others, the supervisor will have to help the employees resolve their disagreement. Frequently though, the cause is something related to the basic nature of the two personalities involved. Even the cleverest supervisors can't change people's personalities. The most they can hope to do is to get the two employees to work reasonably well together despite their admitted personality differences.

One recommended method is to call both parties into a private office. Let both in turn state what they think the problems are and blow off a little steam. Then act as an impartial mediator whose only interest is to keep up production. *You must let these employees know that you will not tolerate the situation as it is.*

Encourage the employees to discuss ways of resolving the problem and to agree on a course of corrective action. Keep a close watch on the situation and call further interviews if warranted. Make sure both employees know what the consequences will be if their negative behaviour continues.

DEALING WITH EMOTIONAL PEOPLE

If we've caused a person to feel badly and he or she reacts emotionally, we normally comfort that person — and rightly so. In the work place, however, you need to keep your distance from staff who become emotional. For example, you may be a supervisor who has the unpleasant task of disciplining, dismissing or laying off an employee. Perhaps the person is in tears and very embarrassed about it. How can you make this situation easier for both people?

One of my tasks when I worked in human resources was the chore of laying off or firing employees. Because I'm a real softy, I would occasionally become emotional along with the person being laid off or disciplined. By accident, I found a way of helping both of us regain our equilibrium.

I achieved this when I handed the person a box of tissues and said, "I have something I have to attend to. I'll be back in a few minutes." Then I left the room and took a few deep breaths. When I felt I had my emotions under control, I went back to my office.

Because I had given the person the same opportunity to calm down, she had regained her composure and some of her self-respect. We were able to continue the conversation until we took care of all the issues.

Save using this tactic for situations that warrant it. Many people use tears to get sympathy and will try to manipulate you with their tears. When dealing with this type, I give them a box of tissues and continue the conversation.

DEALING WITH RACIAL AND ETHNIC SLURS
Most work forces, if they're in compliance with the law, are a mixture of individuals of different backgrounds. Companies show poor management if they ignore or tolerate a racial or ethnic slur against an employee, a supervisor, a customer or a member of the public. Such derogatory language is bad public relations for the company and causes problems between employees.

Jokes at the expense of someone else aren't jokes at all. Managers should never knowingly joke about someone's background or personal appearance or condone such behaviour in their employees. One can't judge on the surface how such a joke might affect an individual. Racial or ethnic slurs stem from prejudice. Prejudice is based on stereotyped views and generalizations about a group and shows a lack of respect for people as individuals.

Supervisors should clearly demonstrate management's attitude towards prejudice by openly showing their disapproval of any racial or ethnic slur. The supervisor may also need to interview the offender privately. The person may insist that his or her comments were harmless. The supervisor's reply should be, "Charlie, they may be *meant* to be harmless, but they have a harmful effect, so keep your thoughts to yourself."

If the problem continues, the supervisor should say, "Charlie, performance appraisals show how employees get along with the other employees and customers. I wouldn't like to place a comment on your file that you don't get along. However, if you continue to make these disparaging remarks, I'll have to place a written warning on your file. Do you understand?"

OTHER SUPERVISORY PROBLEMS
"My front-line people are always referring their difficult clients to me instead of handling them themselves."

Help them acquire the skills they need to deal with these difficult people (give them a copy of this book, perhaps). Explain to them how you expect them to deal with abusive, profane or threatening behaviour. You may instruct them to hang up or to transfer the caller to you.

Often irate clients take all their irritability out on clerical staff and are as sweet as pie with supervisors or managers. Don't assume that your clerical staff were exaggerating about the unpleasant behaviour of the client. Identify what is and is not acceptable client behaviour. Support your staff when they've been mistreated. Explain to the client, "We don't tolerate harassment of our staff. I suggest you apologize to Margie about the way you spoke to her."

"Top management says we can bend the rules for special clients. My staff objects."

I don't blame them. Nothing is as annoying as saying no to clients who then go over your head, and persuade someone higher up to say yes. Support your staff by talking to your manager. Ask for some hard and fast rules. Explain the difficulties that have resulted. Give concrete examples, demonstrating the costs in hard feelings, poor morale, etc. The better you're prepared before you confront management, the less chance there will be that they'll turn you down. If management does turn down your request, explain what has happened to your staff.

"How can I help my staff feel comfortable when they have to enforce unpopular rules and regulations?"

Teach them the "stuck-record" technique. Request that they use this technique without raising their voices, or showing annoyance of any kind. Help them develop the necessary responses, such as, "I'm sorry. I'd like to make an exception in your case, but I can't bend the rules for anyone." Instruct them to repeat the relevant form of words as often as necessary. Be ready to back them up if someone attempts to go over their head.

"How can I handle having to cut staff, which makes four people do the work of five?"

This becomes necessary when the economy forces companies to "tighten their belts." If you haven't taken a time mangement course, now's the time to do so. It will teach you how to set priorities and concentrate on the most important tasks. In doing so you will set a good example for your staff. If you help your subordinates to use good time management techniques, you may find that four people *can* do the work of five and do so effectively.

Learn to cut corners, and try new methods for completion of tasks. Have meetings with your staff to discuss easier, quicker ways of doing tasks. Listen to their ideas carefully. Because they're the ones who are actually doing the tasks, they often come up with the best time-saving suggestions.

"My staff is always misinterpreting my instructions."

Use the paraphrasing technique to check that they have understood what you want. This technique is most effective when you're giving instructions or training someone. It will confirm to you that they "heard what you said." Be careful when asking for paraphrasing that you don't make it sound as if you think they're too dumb to understand your instructions. It is your responsibility to be sure your instructions are clear, not theirs to interpret a confusing message.

"My staff want me to spend my valuable time answering their unimportant questions."

Many supervisors may get mad at interruptions, but many others inadvertently encourage helplessness in their subordinates. When an employee comes to them with a problem, some supervisors immediately provide the solution. It would be better if they first asked, "What do you think you should do about this?" It's surprising how often the employee does know what to do. This strategy encourages independent thinking by employees. When they realize that they often have the answers already, and that you support them, they'll have more faith in their own judgment in the future.

If subordinates really don't know the answer, by all means help them. That's what you're there for.

"I hate disciplining my staff!"

It's possible that you weren't trained properly for your supervisory position. Get this training so you'll feel more comfortable when giving discipline. Remember that everything your subordinates do makes *you* look good or bad. If you allow them to do careless work, you'll be setting yourself up for a reprimand yourself. The aim of discipline is to correct poor productivity or behaviour problems, not to instil a desire to retaliate in the employee. Discipline, done correctly, moves the guilt from the shoulders of the supervisor onto those of the person being disciplined. The employee is told what the consequences will be if the unacceptable behaviour continues. I repeat: get supervisory training — especially in the area of employee discipline!

"I'm not quite ready to retire. How do I handle the 'heel-nippers' who want my job?"

This is tough. You don't want to move to the next level, but you shouldn't try to stop those who are young and eager from progressing. Suggest to them that they try another department and go around your position. Do everything in your power to get them ready for when you're ready to retire. If this is within two years, don't worry about the people behind you. Don't hamper them from being ready for your job or you'll just have unhappy, vindictive subordinates.

If you prove to them that you're interested not only in your own welfare, but also in theirs, they'll probably be more patient. They'll feel more comfortable if they know there will be an end to their waiting. Make it clear to them what your plans are. Explain that you're going to retire in two years. If it's longer than two years, you're probably going to spend the remainder of your employment bored to tears. If this is the case, keep working towards a more senior position yourself.

"My staff expect me to use all their bright ideas."

Judge every new idea on its own merits. Explain your conclusions, if there is some reason why it won't work. If there's some value to the idea, explain why you can or can't use the idea at that particular time. Keep encouraging your staff to come up with new ideas. After all, aren't they the ones who are actually carrying on the activities? If you stop their ideas, you'll just be demotivating them, which is the opposite of what you want.

"I have an employee who balks and wants to do things her way."

Whenever you have the ability to do so, allow your staff to complete tasks "their" way. If there's no room for flexibility in how a task is completed, be clear in your instructions. Explain that your instructions will bring about the results you want. If your employee continues to argue, ask her, "Are you refusing to do this task the way I want you do to it?" If she says, "Yes," you could rightfully charge her with insubordination. Try other methods first, but know that your only recourse may be to place a formal written warning on her file.

"My employee is very people-oriented, but is terribly disorganized. When left unsupervised he's on the phone for hours."

Use this person to make oral presentations and to deal directly with clients. Give careful, detailed instructions on what you want from him. Make sure his job description is up to date, giving standards of performance, and timelines for completion of tasks. Explain that he should not be making personal telephone calls. Initiate discipline and explain the consequences if the phone calls continue.

"My secretary is a perfectionist in everything she does, even when it's wasting valuable time. She seems to keep herself buried in her own work, doesn't seem aware of things going on around her. Because of this, she doesn't understand how her actions affect others in the department."

Give her deadlines to meet and explain the results you expect. Send her to a time management course. If you need a draft copy of something, make sure she understands that typing errors are allowed, etc. Give her information that explains how her position fits in with others in the department. This could be by showing her a copy of the organizational chart of your section or department. Explain that when she is late with her work, it has a direct effect on others. "Margaret, when your month-end report is late, it holds up our whole department's month-end report."

"Should I be socializing with my staff?"

If you used to work with your subordinates, this may be a tough problem to solve. Remind yourself that you now have a new peer group and should be socializing with other supervisors, not your subordinates. I'm not saying you can't have coffee breaks with your staff, but don't socialize with only one or two of your staff. If you bowl with one of your subordinates, the others expect you to show favouritism to your "bowling buddy." If you *do* decide to socialize with subordinates, never discuss business! That's not fair to the other members of your staff.

ARE YOU READY FOR SUCCESS?

You now have the tools that will enable you to deal with irate, rude, impatient, emotional, upset, persistent and aggressive people. These essential people skills will help you to handle all types of difficult individuals and situations. Learn these skills, and you can't help but improve your relationships with staff, superiors, co-workers and clients. Because these skills are now so important to businesses, this can lead to better assignments, promotions, more managerial responsibility and overall improvement in employee morale.

Your people skills will help you to control your moods and keep cool under fire. Instead of becoming defensive when dealing with an irate customer, you'll concentrate on solving the client's problem. In the end both of you will be winners.

You'll:

— be a more positive person and have more time to do what *you* want instead of scurrying around trying to placate others;
— be able to deal with angry or aggressive clients;
— have the skills to deal with your own anger and stress;
— be able to resist being coerced, manipulated or intimidated by the underhanded methods some people use to get their way. You'll also be able to identify and deal with the underlying problems;
— be a skilful negotiator, adept at conflict resolution;
— know how to interpret and use non-verbal signals;

- be able to identify your own and others' passive, aggressive and assertive behaviour;
- know how to say no without feeling guilty;
- know how to use your communication skills to improve your effectiveness as a client, co-worker, employee or supervisor;
- know how to deal with personality clashes;
- understand the use of feedback to ensure that others are aware of how you feel about both the good and bad things they're doing;
- know how to use paraphrasing to confirm that what you heard was really what was said;
- obtain more praise and approval from your associates because you can now control your negative feelings.

Learn the techniques and practise them daily. They *do* work! Like any new skill, however, they need to be used consistently until they're automatic. When you've mastered them, you can look forward to being able to control how you deal with and react to others.

No longer will you allow others to decide what kind of day you have. Because you have gained this control, your self-esteem will rise. The more confident you are, the less stress and anxiety you'll feel and the more energy and enthusiasm you can bring to all aspects of your life. If you use these skills, you'll need to be prepared for success, because success *will* inevitably follow!

APPENDIX

Job advice

Business and Technician Education
Council (BTEC)
Central House
Upper Woburn Place
London WC1H
Tel: 071–388 3288

Careers Research Advisory Centre
(CRAC)
Sheraton House
Castle Park
Cambridge CB3 0AX
Tel: 0223 460277

Department of Employment
OB2 Caxton House
Tothill Street
London SW1H 9HA
Tel: 071–273 3000

Department of Trade and Industry
1–19 Victoria Street
London SW1H
Tel: 071–215 5000

Manpower Services Commission
Training Division
MSC
Moorfoot
Sheffield S1 4PQ
Tel: 0742 753275

Careers and Occupational
Information Centre (COIC)
MSC
Moorfoot
Sheffield S1 4PQ
Tel: 0742 753275

Information, advice and rights

ACAS
Head Office
27 Wilton Street
London SW1X 7AZ
Tel: 071–210 3000

Ask for your regional office.

Equal Opportunities Commission
(EOC)
Overseas House
Quay Street
Manchester M3 3HN
Tel: 061–833 9244

Rights of Women
52–54 Featherstone Street
London EC1Y 8RT
Tel: 071–251 6577

TUC Equal Rights Department
Congress House
Great Russell Street
London WC1
Tel: 071–636 4030

BIBLIOGRAPHY

Auerback, Sylvia. "Difficult Co-workers — Handle with Care." *Computer Decisions* 13 (Dec. 1981), 178 ff.

Berne, Eric. *Games People Play*. London: Penguin 1970.

Bernstein, Albert J., and Sydney Craft Rosen. *Dinosaur Brains*. New York: John Wiley and Sons, 1989.

Bramson, Robert M. *Coping with Difficult People*. New York: Ballantine Books, 1981.

Carnegie, Dale. *How to Win Friends and Influence People*. London: Heinemann, 1986.

Elgin, Suzette Haden. *The Last Word on the Gentle Art of Verbal Self-defense*. New York: Prentice-Hall, 1987.

Farley, Lin. *Sexual Shakedown: The Sexual Harassment of Women on the Job*. New York: McGraw-Hill, 1978.

Filley, Allan C. *Interpersonal Conflict Resolution*. Glenview, Ill.: Scott, Foresman, 1975.

Freudenberger, H.J., and G. Richelson. *Burnout*. New York: Doubleday, 1980.

Gordon, Thomas. *P.E.T.: Parent Effectiveness Training*. New York: New American Library, 1970.

Hall, Edward T. *The Silent Language*. New York: Anchor Press, 1988. Available from Ashgrove Distribution.

Levinson, Harry. *Executive Stress*. Harvard Business School Press, 1988.

Smith, Manuel J. *When I Say No, I Feel Guilty*. London: Bantam Books, 1976.

Weisinger, Hendrie, and Norman M. Lobsenz. *Nobody's Perfect: How To Give Criticism and Get Results*. Los Angeles: Stradford Press, 1981.

Ziegenfuss, James T., Jr. "Responding to People Problems." *Business Horizons* 23 (Apr. 1980), 73–76.

Business Books for Successful Managers

PIATKUS BUSINESS BOOKS have been created for people like you, busy executives and managers who need expert knowledge readily available in a clear and easy-to-follow format. All the books are written by specialists in their field. They will help you improve your skills quickly and effortlessly in the workplace and on a personal level.

Each book is packed with ideas and good advice which can be put into practice immediately. Titles include:

The Best Person for the Job Malcolm Bird

Beware the Naked Man Who Offers You His Shirt Harvey Mackay

The Complete Time Management System Christian H. Godefroy and John Clark

Dealing with Difficult People Roberta Cava

The Energy Factor: How to Motivate Your Workforce Art McNeil

How to Become Rich and Successful Charles Templeton

How to Close Every Sale Joe Girard with Robert L. Shook

How to Collect the Money You are Owed Malcolm Bird

How to Develop and Profit from Your Creative Powers Michael LeBoeuf

How to Win Customers and Keep Them for Life Michael LeBoeuf

Leadership Skills for Every Manager Jim Clemmer and Art McNeil

Powerspeak: The Complete Guide to Public Speaking and Communication Dorothy Leeds

Smart Questions for Successful Managers Dorothy Leeds

The Strategy of Meetings George David Kieffer

Your Memory Kenneth L. Higbee

You too can benefit from expert advice. Just look out for our distinctive Piatkus silver business book jackets in the shops. For a free brochure with further information on our complete range of business titles, please write to:

Business Books Department
Piatkus Books
5 Windmill Street
London, W1P 1HF

PIATKUS

HOW TO WIN CUSTOMERS AND KEEP THEM FOR LIFE
by Michael LeBoeuf

How to Win Customers and Keep Them for Life will be the most important sales aid you will ever have. It will tell you:

- How to provide the best quality customer service
- The reasons which makes customers buy and come back
- How to be the kind of person customers like to buy from
- How to find more customers
- How to make customers recognise the fine service you give them
- The five best ways to keep customers coming back
- How to keep your customers happy

How to Win Customers and Keep Them for Life is a hard-hitting, action-ready, rewards and incentive programme for creating a winning sales team. Written by Michael LeBoeuf, one of America's foremost business consultants, this practical no-nonsense guide tells you everything you need to know about successful selling.

THE BEST PERSON FOR THE JOB
by Malcolm Bird

This comprehensive book is packed with advice on where to find the best person for the job – and how to keep that person happy and working effectively. It explains how to:

- Assess your company's needs
- Look for the right person yourself
- Write a suitable job advertisement
- Make the best use of agencies and consultants
- Deal with applications
- Interview applicants
- Work out the right rate for the job
- Get your successful candidate started
- Keep your employees happy and enthusiastic
- Deal with absenteeism
- Handle the situation if things go wrong

Malcolm Bird is a management consultant and the author of several books.

THE COMPLETE TIME MANAGEMENT SYSTEM
by Christian H. Godefroy and John Clark

The Complete Time Management System will change the way you work and think. It will increase your enjoyment of life and your chances of success. It will show you:

- How to do in 2 hours what you usually need 4 hours to do
- How to revive your concentration
- How to read 240 pages an hour – with better understanding and memorisation
- How to make an important decision faster
- How to delegate
- How to organise your office
- How to shorten meetings
- And much, much more

Learn the secrets of time management and you will profit from them all your life.

Christian Godefroy is a training specialist, founder of a publishing company in France, and best-selling author.

HOW TO COLLECT THE MONEY YOU ARE OWED
by Malcolm Bird

Getting paid on time is vital for any business. In *How to Collect the Money You are Owed*, Malcom Bird gives practical advice on how to organise your invoicing and money collecting systems, improve your cash flow and increase your profitability.

- Learn how to control your cash flow cycle
- Develop an efficient invoicing system
- Get to know your clients and how they operate
- Learn how to chase up money effectively
- Discover what to do if all else fails

How to Collect the Money You are Owed will help you save time and money. It is an essential handbook for every office.

Malcolm Bird is a management consultant and the author of several books.